Seven Essays on Populism

Critical South

The publication of this series is supported by the International Consortium of Critical Theory Programs funded by the Andrew W. Mellon Foundation.

Series editors: Natalia Brizuela and Leticia Sabsay

Seven Essays on Populism

For a Renewed Theoretical Perspective

Paula Biglieri and Luciana Cadahia

Translated by George Ciccariello-Maher

polity

Excerpt from the article "The Populist Challenge to Liberal Democracy" by William Galston, *Journal of Democracy* 29:2 (2018), 5–19. © 2018 National Endowment for Democracy and the Johns Hopkins University Press. Reprinted with permission of Johns Hopkins University Press.

Excerpt from the article "How populist uprisings could bring down liberal democracy" by Yascha Mounk, *The Guardian*, March 2018 © Guardian News & Media Ltd 2020. Reprinted with permission of *The Guardian*.

Polity Press
65 Bridge Street
Cambridge CB2 1UR, UK

Polity Press
101 Station Landing
Suite 300
Medford, MA 02155, USA

ISBN-13: 978-1-5095-4220-8 – hardback
ISBN-13: 978-1-5095-4221-5 – paperback

A catalogue record for this book is available from the British Library.
Library of Congress Cataloging-in-Publication Data

Names: Biglieri, Paula, author. | Cadahia, Luciana, 1982- author.
Title: Seven essays on populism : for a renewed theoretical perspective / Paula Biglieri and Luciana Cadahia ; translated by George Ciccariello-Maher.
Description: English Edition. | Medford : Polity Press, 2021. | Series: Critical South | Includes bibliographical references and index. | Summary: "A critical exploration of the meaning and potential of populism in contemporary political thought"-- Provided by publisher.
Identifiers: LCCN 2020027959 (print) | LCCN 2020027960 (ebook) | ISBN 9781509542208 (Hardback) | ISBN 9781509542215 (Paperback) | ISBN 9781509542222 (ePub) | ISBN 9781509547029 (Adobe PDF)
Subjects: LCSH: Populism.
Classification: LCC JC423 .B53 2021 (print) | LCC JC423 (ebook) | DDC 320.56/62--dc23
LC record available at https://lccn.loc.gov/2020027959
LC ebook record available at https://lccn.loc.gov/2020027960

Typeset in 10.5 on 12.5pt Sabon
by Fakenham Prepress Solutions, Fakenham, Norfolk NR21 8NL
Printed and bound in Great Britain by TJ Books Limited

The publisher has used its best endeavors to ensure that the URLs for external websites referred to in this book are correct and active at the time of going to press. However, the publisher has no responsibility for the websites and can make no guarantee that a site will remain live or that the content is or will remain appropriate.

Every effort has been made to trace all copyright holders, but if any have been overlooked the publisher will be pleased to include any necessary credits in any subsequent reprint or edition.

For further information on Polity, visit our website:
politybooks.com

Tarsila do Amaral (1886–1973) is one of the most prominent representatives of Latin American modernism and one of the most renowned artists in Brazil. Her work *Abaporu*, 1928, inspired the Anthropophagic Movement in the plastic arts. To learn more: www.tarsiladoamaral.com.br.

Her work *Operários*, 1933, is featured on the cover of this book and was created during the social phase of the artist's work, after she returned from Russia.

Contents

Stand up, you who know how to feel and do not suffer the painful frigidity of academics.

Jorge Eliécer Gaitán

Foreword

Wendy Brown

Democracies are generally thought to die at the barrel of a gun, in coups and revolutions. These days, however, they are more likely to be strangled slowly in the name of the people.

The Economist, August 2019

... leftist populism is a profound error. It has no chance of matching the populist appeal of the right, and it dangerously validates some of the right's arguments.

Tony Blair, *The New York Times*, March 2017

There can no longer be any doubt that we are going through a populist moment. The question is whether this populist moment will turn into a populist age – and cast the very survival of liberal democracy in doubt.

Yascha Mounk, *The Guardian*, March 2018

The People vs. Democracy

Title of Yascha Mounk's 2018 book

When populists distinguish between the "people" and the "elite," they depict each of these groups as homogeneous. Populism is the enemy of pluralism, and thus of modern democracy.

William Galston, "The Populist Challenge to Liberal Democracy"[1]

Mainstream political discourse today, both scholarly and journalistic, equates populism with hard-right mobilizations animated by zealous passion born of resentment and led by irresponsible demagogues. Populism is presumed anti-liberal in every sense of the word, as well as disdainful of Constitutionalism, universalism, limited state power, and democratic institutions. The discourse also holds populism responsible for bringing to power authoritarian, ethno-nationalist regimes around the globe, threatening the disintegration of the European Union and endangering the civilizing and civilized reign of liberal democratic values. It is figured as rightist in essence, or, as the case of Venezuela is believed to demonstrate, as inevitably turning autocratic or despotic.[2] It is cast as embodying a simplistic and binaristic worldview, feeding on economic and cultural vulnerability, and rejecting facticity, truth, and expertise, as well as inclusion, pluralism, and tolerance.[3] It is ugly to the core.

This vilification of populism is not unique to the present moment. Rather, Biglieri and Cadahia teach us in this rich and erudite work, populism has always been in disrepute. This is true in Europe where right-wing populism requires no modifier, and left or democratic populism are oxymorons. It is true in the United States, notwithstanding its rich history of populist rebellion against control of local and national government by financial elites. It is true in Latin America, where populism is associated with Peronism *and* socialism, neoliberalism *and* Chavismo. Populism, Biglieri and Cadahia remind us, has been disparaged by liberals and Marxists, globalists and institutionalists, social engineers and free-marketeers, oligarchic republicans and egalitarian social democrats, colonial managers and their postcolonial elite successors. It has been charged with deviating from true class struggle, symptomizing mal-development or failure to modernize, expressing social-psychic primitivism or regression to the mob, rebelling against democratic constraints and institutions, assaulting liberal universalism and inclusion, abhorring cosmopolitanism and globalism, and rebuffing expert and technical knowledge.

As the malignancies discursively associated with populism proliferate and diversify, how might we read this overdetermined outrage and see what it unwillingly confesses? Perhaps, Biglieri and Cadahia declare, populism's threatening force carries an emancipatory secret, "the secret of the people" (1). Perhaps the horror of populism carries a horror of the people, especially of a politics of the people, the power of the people, real democracy. This is the suspicion that animates *Seven Essays on Populism*, a work situated in the history and politics of Latin America but fashioned from a richly international theoretical arsenal. This suspicion fuels the authors' twofold bid to defend populism against all comers and to address populism's internal challenges – its potential complicity with neoliberalism, exclusionary nationalisms, authoritarian leaders, mob affect, machismo, and more. Thus, a book that begins by cleaning centuries of mud from its object develops by helping that object meet contemporary political challenges. Biglieri and Cadahia want to redeem populism, to be sure, but also to contribute to its theoretical and political development for 21st-century "militant" left struggles.[4]

A theoretical orientation and apparatus are immensely helpful when undertaking a task of this magnitude. Theory helps to parse the sloppy ways the term has been bandied about, and to diagnose the hyperbole and the metonymic slide between its pejorative associations –"the aesthetically ugly, the morally evil, a lack of civic culture, contempt for institutions, [rife with] demagoguery, and irrationality" (4). Theory permits critical analysis of populism's identification with historical backwardness and "regression," revealing the conceits of modernity, modernization theory, and Orientalism on which this identification draws (5). Theory permits an *exposé* of the philosophical premises and political frames of liberal and left critiques of populism. Above all, theory permits Biglieri and Cadahia to formulate what they term the logics – rather than only the empirics – of populism, and thus disrupts the casual epistemological positivism fueling much of its opposition and securing the intellectual confidence of its enemies.

Biglieri and Cadahia are rigorous and imaginative theorists in their own right. They are also dedicated students of philosopher Ernesto Laclau, whom they identify as the first and most important contemporary thinker to lift populism from the dirt and make it central to rethinking the nature of "the political." Through his own writing and the collaborative academic sites he helped to create in Essex and Buenos Aires, Laclau bore down on the "excess" that populism is always accused of generating to discover logics in that excess that precisely challenge the logics of liberalism and, later, neoliberalism. Populism, Laclau showed, challenges the liberal logics by which citizenship is always imagined individualized, power is imagined appropriately institutionalized, problems are imagined isolated from one another, and democratic popular sovereignty is reduced to voting and representation. Populism contests each of these as it brings into being "the people" in place of the citizen or voter; a "frontier" of contest between the people and the elite in place of isolated social problems; a "populist rupture" in place of referral of problems to institutions; and a counter-hegemonic struggle for a different order in place of popular sovereignty identified with parliamentary democracy.

For Laclau, these challenges to liberal political logics do not mean that populism is anti-democratic or assaults democracy. Rather, populism radicalizes expectations of and forms for democracy as it explodes liberal democratic fictions of institutional (and linguistic) neutrality and depoliticized social problems. Far from attacking democracy, populism for Laclau (and his sometimes co-author Chantal Mouffe) entails democracy's radicalization and its dissemination beyond the formally political to domains conventionally designated as social and economic. Populism permits extension of democratic critiques and democratic demands to those subjected or excluded across a range of identities and experiences. Populism rejects both the (Marxist) reduction of oppression to class and the (liberal) reduction of exclusion or inequality to absent rights.

Let us take this more slowly. Far from being inherently right-wing reaction, for Laclau populism comprises a set of logics, a set of principles and a set of critiques. Above all, for Laclau, populism reveals "the ontology of the political." By this, Laclau does not mean that populist content is the *Ur* spirit of politics, its ultimate truth and meaning. Nor does he mean that either populism or the political have fixed foundations or essential elements. On the contrary, Laclau's insistence on populism's revelation of the ontology of the political is relentlessly postfoundational; it corresponds to the absence of foundations and essences in political life. Far from being found in God, nature, reason or axioms of history, all political claims and formations are created, generated from militancy aspiring to hegemony. And populism's subject, "the people," is itself an empty signifier – articulated, rather than found or given, and irreducible to any specific population.

Populism's status as the ontology of the political, then, correlates populism's alleged "shiftiness" with the lack of foundations, fixed significations, and strict referents in the political. Thus, Laclau retorts to the charges that populism comprises vague, affective, and rhetorical discourse: "instead of counter-posing 'vagueness' to a mature political logic ... we should start asking ourselves ... 'is not the "vagueness" of populist discourses the consequence of social reality itself being, in some situations, vague and undetermined?'" (Laclau, 2005a: 17). Instead of condemning populism's "rhetorical excesses" and simplifications, he suggests, populism reveals rhetoric as fundamental to political life and at the heart of the constitution of political identities (2005a: 18–19). Instead of treating the eruption of politicized social demands as a dangerous disruption to liberal democratic norms – as a political malady – populism reveals social antagonisms as at the basis of all politics.

For Laclau, then, far from being a fallen form of politics, "populism is the royal road to understanding something about the ontological constitution of the political as such" (2005a: 67). We might also put this the other way around. Through the lens of populism, we can see just how profoundly anti-political much of Western political life and political theory has been. From Platonism and Marxism through liberalism and neoliberalism, most theory and practice aims at taming, reducing or disavowing the qualities of the political overtly expressed in populism – antagonism, rhetoric, constituted identity, indeterminacy and, above all, the power of the people. Most political theory and practice in the Western tradition has aimed at extinguishing these elements and instead identified "management of community [as] the concern of an administrative power whose source of legitimacy is a proper knowledge of what a 'good' community is" (2005a: x). Exceptions to this anti-political orientation are few and rare. There is Machiavelli, with his subtle appreciation of political drama, effect and affect, of invented formations and alliances, and his recognition that the health of republics, far from being endangered by popular "tumults," is secured by them. There is Tocqueville, writing in the democratic (as opposed to oligarchic) republican tradition, who grasped the value for democracy – along with the messiness – of cultivating an energized people ambitious to share political power for purposes beyond pursuit of individual or class interests. And there is Gramsci, that ardent student of Machiavelli and not only Marx, who theorized the importance of actively linking popular struggles to articulate a new hegemonic bloc. Today, there are also left Schmittians, Deleuzians, and radical democrats, but they hold a tellingly small place in contemporary political theory, where liberal approaches reiterate the long tradition of attempting to expunge from politics contingency, fabrication, rhetoric, antagonism, agonism, and the popular – all that constitutes the political from a populist perspective.

Biglieri and Cadahia broadly endorse Laclau's identification of populism with the ontology of the political. They focus especially on the aspect of this identification that features the transformation of different social antagonisms into allied political ones. As a politics that is explicitly made not born, a politics that does not express these social antagonisms directly and individually but, rather, actively (militantly) crafts them into a hegemonic formation opposing powerlessness to power, populism invents a new dividing line and the identities on both sides of it: "the underdog" versus the "power" in Laclau's words, "the people versus the enemies of the people" in those of Biglieri and Cadahia (16). Here, they pursue Laclau's alertness to populism's unique alchemical capacity to transform segmented, siloed, or what he called *differential* demands into an *equivalential* relation with one another. This is the transformation that de-individuates these demands, developing instead a political *frontier* between the people and the power, a frontier that in turn opens new political possibilities and imaginaries. This is the alchemy that permits a critical perspective on and challenge to the discourse, organization, and arrangements, not merely the distributions, of the status quo. This is an alchemy that explodes the limits of the interest group pluralism of liberalism and the class politics of Marxism while remaining legible to and in present discourses. Therein lies populism's deep immediate radical potential.

As they pursue this line of thinking, populism emerges not merely as *a* but *the* political form capable of challenging liberal individualization and depoliticization in the present. As it releases interests and identities from their silos, it substantively links – without dissolving – these identities to form a counter-hegemony that indicts the status quo and opposes the *political* power securing it. Populism reconfigures the excluded and dispossessed as articulating "different demands with one another until achieving an equivalential chain capable of challenging the status quo and establishing a frontier between those on the bottom (the articulated people) and those on top (the status quo)" (14). The "people" or the "plebs," previously discounted, fragmented, and separated from each other, at once claim representation of the whole and politicize their exclusion (16).

In the United States, the best recent exemplar of the populist alchemy Biglieri and Cadahia are theorizing is not the white Americans constituting Trump's base of support in 2016, but the 99% of the Occupy Movement earlier in the decade. The 99% comprised all sectors of labor, people of color, the indebted, the indigenous, the unbanked, the undocumented, the unhoused, the under-educated, the overcharged, the poor, working, and middle classes. The 99% was not a class, an identity or even an intentional coalition. Nor was its opposition only the state, the bosses, the bankers, the corporations or the rich. Rather, the 99% designated a people excluded, exploited, bilked, and disenfranchised; the "power" it opposed was the plutocrats. The 99% and the 1% identified the losers and winners of neoliberalism, privatization, financialization, and government bailouts in the aftermath of the 2008–9 financial crisis. The 99% included democracy itself and the well-being of the planet; the 1% extended to the Supreme Court majority and the international Davos crowd.[5] Everything plundered, devalued or made precarious by capitalist plutocracy was linked in the aspirational hegemonic bloc of the 99%.

If Laclau's bold move to identify populism with the political is troubled by the difficulty of stipulating *the political*, he surely succeeds in recovering populism from its derogatory associations to reveal its insurrectionary and radical democratic potential. However, more still is needed to unfasten it decisively from right-wing popular mobilizations supporting authoritarian leaders or regimes, and especially from ethno-nationalism and fascism. This unfastening is the key aim of Biglieri and Cadahia's work. To achieve it, they carefully elaborate and dismantle the premises undergirding mainstream and left anti-populist critiques, including those of Eric Fassin, Slavoj Žižek, and Maurizio Lazzarato. They also critically analyze the claims of closer allies – Chantal Mouffe, Oliver Marchart and Yannis Stavrakakis – that populism may take right-wing forms but is equally available to left, emancipatory, another-world-is-possible democratic demands. Going a remarkable step further, Biglieri and Cadahia argue that populism is only left, only radically democratic, only anti-authoritarian, only the final and full realization of equality, liberty, universality, and community. Populism, they argue, is *the* emancipatory revolutionary theory and practice for our time. Conversely, what pundits call "populism" ought to be called by its true name: fascism.

Only left populism is populism, all other movements in the name of "the people" are fascist – how is such a claim possible? How, especially, can it be developed from a Laclauian formulation of populism in which "the people" is an empty signifier – always rhetorically designated, always a part representing the whole, always brought into being through articulations in every sense of the word? And how does this argument square with the worldwide eruption of what almost everyone calls authoritarian populism? How can these reactionary formations be purged from the populist treasure chest, and how is left populism purged of its persistent flirtation with non-democratic practices, especially given its connection to strong leaders and uncompromising demands?

The arguments Biglieri and Cadahia develop for this claim depend upon but exceed Laclau's. For Biglieri and Cadahia, the equivalential relation that Laclau establishes as constitutive of a populist formation is sustained only when equality is achieved through heterogeneity, through embrace rather than expulsion or erasure of differences. They cite Jorge Alemán: "The *pueblo* is an unstable equivalence constituted by differences that never unify or represent the whole" (2016: 21). The people, they insist, is brought into being not through unification or homogenized difference but only through antagonism to the elite or dominant power. If heterogeneity is constitutive of a populist formation, then only by sustaining it does populism remain populism; only by sustaining it does "the people" remain an emancipatory formulation that insists on equality and justice for all.

Right-wing popular formations, by contrast, suppress difference to make and assert the "one people." Right-wing formations make identity and equality dependent on suppression of difference internally, and exclusion of difference externally (38). Here drawing on Bataille, Biglieri and Cadahia insist that what distinguishes populism from right-wing popular movements is the latter's fantasy of the homogeneity that signifies both "the commensurability of elements and [political] awareness of this commensurability" (39). Commensurability of elements and the unity and oneness it achieves depend on identifying equality with sameness and inequality with difference. Because it "involves the violence of trying to dissolve the play of difference–equivalence into a broader identity ... a self-transparent people," it is an *essentially* repressive and violent formulation and formation (39). To return to Laclau's terms, the commensurability of elements, and the equality and unity staged through this commensurability, is fundamentally at odds with the equivalential logic or premise of populism. The right-wing "fantasy of the one-people that contains the longing for a life without problems or antagonisms within the tranquility of a homogeneous social space" cannot tolerate the "constitutive differences of the articulatory logic of populism" (39). Then, Biglieri and Cadahia wonder, "should we continue to call it populism, especially when the classic term 'fascism' exists?" (39). Their answer is definitive. What the pundits call authoritarian populism is no populism at all.

Having ripped away populism from right-wing popular formations, two projects remain. One is to unthread populism from its potential solicitude toward, and imbrication with, neoliberalism, nationalism, authoritarian leadership, state centrism, anti-institutionalism, and naturalism. The other is to connect populism decisively to socialism, feminism, radical democracy, popular sovereignty, international solidarity, ethics, and a politics of care. This is what Biglieri and Cadahia do across the last five essays of the book.

By now, the reader's curiosity is piqued – how do they do it? – but also likely suspicious about the grandness, even grandiosity, of the project. It is one thing to redeem populism from ignorant punditry, anxious liberalism, colonial and modernization frames, or condemnations by unreconstructed Marxists. It is another to make populism so righteous, so complete, always landing on the correct square of every contemporary political challenge. Have Biglieri and Cadahia perhaps offered a new political theology, a political form both perfect in itself and inherently insulated from all that might compromise or sully it? If the political domain is open in signification, composition and direction, if it has no historical necessity and is rife with contingency, how and why would or could populist uprisings have such perfection and immunity? If the domain of politics is a realm of contingency, "without guarantees," open to eruptions and alterations – if empty signifiers like "the people," "freedom" or "feminism" can chime with many possible meanings – what does it mean to arrest this openness, these slides, with arguments about populism's inherent ideational logics? Indeed, what does it mean to bring logics to this realm at all? Or to insist on populism's insulation from dark forces through its logics? How can any political paradigm or formation be secured from imbrications with violence? Or escape the re-significations or inversions produced by genealogical fusions and transmogrifications? How do *theoretical* stipulations secure an object in a domain that does not submit to them? Or, to shift the register from Foucault and Gramsci to Weber, if the domain of the political is where ends and means have no necessary relation, and where certain political means easily overwhelm or subdue the ends they are adduced to serve, what protects populism against these things?

In short, have Biglieri and Cadahia not gone too far, overplayed the hand they meant to win? Have they not pressed past their compelling redemption of the potential of left populism to insist that populism alone holds the promise of an emancipatory politics in the twenty-first century? Is there, perhaps, a confession of illegitimate desire here? A desire for populism to be not only "the royal road to understanding the political," as Laclau argued, but the royal road to the Good, the True, and the Beautiful in politics ... and, hence, beyond the political after all?

Still, we would do well to remember that most political concepts invite something of this kind from their partisans, both inside and outside political theory. Hence the many textual and activist efforts to redeem liberalism from its corruscation by neoliberalism, by right-wing libertarianism or by authoritarians. Or to distinguish democracy from market democracy, social democracy or even liberal democracy. Or to distinguish true communism from its repressive state form, or preserve feminism from its bourgeois or imperialist mode. From the protest chant, "this is what democracy looks like!" to scholarly identification of democracy with anti-populist norms and institutions by Levitsky and Ziblatt, to insistence on democracy's agonistic nature by Mouffe, and its fugitive nature by Wolin, there is relentless normative *stipulation* of concepts in political theory and practice. That is what we do with open concepts, with sliding signification, when, as Stuart Hall reminds us, efforts to arrest that slide are at the heart of political struggle. If these are routine practices in politically invested political theory, even – and, perhaps, especially – in genres cloaking themselves in analytic objectivity yet deeply invested in liberalism, why deny this cleansing and redemption for populism? Especially if we remember the founding frame of Biglieri and Cadahia's work – namely, that such a cleansing and redemption of populism is symptomatically refused by all who fear the power of the people, the politics of the people.

Let us try the question differently then. Readers would be counseled to ask not whether Biglieri and Cadahia's formulations of populism's inherently emancipatory force squares with "actually existing populism" (a historical–empirical question), or whether their identification of populism with the Good fully squares with a theory of the political foregrounding absent foundations, contingency and empty or floating signifiers. Rather, let us ask only whether Biglieri and Cadahia, as politically engaged political theorists, have developed a persuasive political theory of populism's inherent and possible qualities, logics, limits, and potentials.

To answer this question, two others must be posed. Can a political paradigm, form or ideal be defended or protected on the basis of theoretical logics imputed to it? And can the deficiencies or vulnerabilities of political forms, paradigms or ideals be resolved at the level of theory? The first queries both whether such logics exist at all – whether, indeed, political forms have logics once they are on the ground of the real, rather than the theoretical – and whether political life unfolds in accord with them. The second queries whether political theory, notwithstanding its power to illuminate both the deficiencies and potentials of political life, nonetheless remains distinct from the living topos that it maps. This is not a retort to radical ideals by *realpolitik* – the latter, too, perpetuates a myth about transhistorical political logics. Rather, the problem is one articulated by Max Weber in his challenge to adopting conventional ethics for political life – whether those bound to particular convictions such as Christian virtue or non-violence, or to a particular end state, such as socialism or neoliberalism. For Weber, the problem with both "an ethic of conviction" and "an ethic of absolute ends" is that they ignore the distinctive *ethical irrationality* of the political realm. By this he does not mean that the realm is inherently immoral, but that actions motivated by one set of intentions potentially unleash effects at odds with those intentions, and may even violate them. Principles and paradigms of the Good, once they have entered political life, do not stay with their authorial intentions; politics is a theatre in which motivations are not decisive and have no ethical relationship to effects. For Weber, this does not mean jettisoning ethics but developing an ethical orientation appropriate to a sphere constituted by action, power and contingency, and shadowed continuously by the potential effects of violence. He identifies this orientation as "an ethic of responsibility." Attempting an ethical orientation in political life means being responsible for the effects of one's actions in a contingent, unpredictable sphere – not treating unintended consequences as external to one's ethics. This is as true of individuals as it is of projects: neither can rest on purity of motives or adherence to the theoretical premises or logics. One cannot say: "Because my motivation is emancipation, and I have theoretically purified populism of all non-emancipatory elements, then anti-democratic, authoritarian, nationalist or other chauvinistic elements are no part of the populism I affirm and help create." Theory and the logics it articulates can never clean the hands of actors or pave the course of actual events in political life.

Foucault approaches this problem a bit differently when discussing the absence of a distinctive governmental rationality in socialism, and the tendency to look to a "text" for the answer to this absence:

> [I]f we are so strongly inclined to put to socialism this indiscreet question of truth that we never address to liberalism – "Are you true or are you false?" – it is precisely because socialism lacks an intrinsic governmental rationality, and because it replaces this essential, and still not overcome [absence of] an internal

governmental rationality, with the relationship of conformity to
a text. The relationship of conformity to a text, or to a series of
texts, is charged with concealing this absence of governmental
rationality. A way of reading and interpreting is advanced that
must found socialism and indicate the very limits and possibilities of its potential action, whereas what it really needs is to
define for itself its way of doing things and its way of governing.
I think the importance of the text in socialism is commensurate
with the lacuna constituted by the absence of a socialist art of
government. (2010: 93–4)

Beyond the specific problematic of socialism, it seems to me,
Foucault here offers a warning against seeking a theoretical
substitute for the "arts of government," the form of governing
reason and specific instruments of power, that are part of
any regime. Whether borrowed or *sui generis*, they will be
employed and deployed. This problem, especially the effort to
discover theoretical or textual substitutions for rationalities
and techniques of governing, bears differently on political
populism as a political form than it does on socialism as an
economic one, but it is no less significant for this difference.

We of the meaning-making and theory-building species
also generate world-making forces (religious, cultural,
economic, social, political, technological) that escape
our grasp and steering capacity. The combination yields
a persistent temptation to attempt re-mastery of these
forces with our intellects. Political theorists are especially
vulnerable to trying to conquer with theory the elements of
action, violence, rhetoric, staging, and contingency constitutive of the political. This conceit afflicts formal modelers,
analytic philosophers, and left theorists alike. We persis-
tently confuse theoretical entailments for political logics,
political logics for political truths, and political truths for
politics *tout court*. How might we escape this room of
distorting mirrors while persisting in the intellectual work
of theorizing political life?

These large questions do not answer whether Biglieri and
Cadahia have offered a persuasive account of populism.
They do query whether their brilliant defense of populism
rests on theoretical moves that illuminate political life yet

are not identical with it. I write this at a time of two ground-shifting popular movements in the United States: one brought Donald Trump to power in 2016, and continues to support his neo-fascist "leadership" along with licensing political and social expressions of every kind of supremacism: patriarchal, white, heterosexual, nativist (but not Native), nationalist, and wealth-based. The other, ignited by the George Floyd chapter in the long American history of anti-black policing, vigilantism, and incarceration, has generated sustained anti-racist protests across America and the world. As they demand racial justice, and attack existing institutions for failing to yield it, these protests express the metamorphosis of a social antagonism into a political formation, one in which the People oppose the Power, which Biglieri and Cadahia identify with populism. Broadening well beyond those immediately affected, the uprisings have brought nearly every sector in every region of America to the streets, and may have dealt the final blow to the Trump regime. They embody the trans-formative possibilities of popular resistance and long-term as well as spontaneous organizing, and they are igniting a new political imaginary, one in which entrenched injustices of the status quo spur rather than limit the making of a radically different future.

Introduction

The book that the reader has in their hands does not aim to be a handbook offering basic and definitive definitions of populism and politics. Nor does it claim to be an academic book in the standard sense of the term, since it does not attempt to reinforce the imaginaries of objectivity or value-neutrality associated with academic work. In contrast to these two attitudes, this book is an avowedly militant one in which we embrace our political position as a way of taking responsibility for our own subjective involvement. Moreover, we believe that the crux of honesty and rigor in intellectual work lies precisely here: in being explicit about our locus of enunciation and putting it to the test. If we engage in this provocative gesture to foster debate around a term, especially one as controversial as populism, it is because we have something to say. And what we say comes from our experiences as women, as academics, as Latin Americans, and as political militants traversed by the various antagonisms that, between populism and neoliberalism, have emerged and continue to exist in our region. However, and despite the specific position from which we speak, we do not intend to produce a knowledge that is merely particular, as if our double condition as women and as Latin American means that we can only speak to local and specific problems. Very much to the contrary, our commitment is to attempt to grasp what is universalizable – in the sense of a situated universalism – in the problems, challenges, and responses offered by a locus of enunciation like Latin America within the emancipatory production of knowledge in the Global South and Global North. We are convinced that epistemic decolonization also involves understanding that local problems demand global solutions through the construction of egalitarian academic spaces for debating transformative ideas.

That said, it is worth noting that, when we began to work on populism, the political context in Latin America was broadly favorable to anti-neoliberal, egalitarian, and inclusive discourses geared toward the expansion of rights. The Social Democratic Party (PSD) in Portugal had also been reinvented; experiences like those of SYRIZA, Podemos, and La France Insoumise were born; and a curious popular liberalism had been reactivated in the cases of Jeremy Corbyn and Bernie Sanders, who were fighting for plebeian and egalitarian alternatives in Europe and North America. But since then, and as our research on populism moved forward, the political situation took a major step backward. The ebb of populist experiences in Latin America brought with it the rise of neoliberal governments that not only sought virulently to disarm the egalitarian accomplishments of populism, but also targeted the fundamental premises of the rule of law and democratic coexistence. Latin America has become a political laboratory for testing out different forms of post-democratic life for the capitalism of the future. This translates into disarming our institutional structure through the irresponsible acquisition of foreign debt to the International Monetary Fund or private investment funds, the acceleration of paradoxically democratic soft coups,[1] the judicial persecution and imprisonment of popular leaders through rigged proceedings, political experiments based on dehistoricization, new age philosophies, and social coaching, and the alarming rise in the systematic murder of social activists. Regarding soft coups, it is worth highlighting the recent coup against Evo Morales in Bolivia during the most recent presidential elections in 2019, and the institutional coup perpetrated against Brazilian President Dilma Rousseff in 2016. The latter strategy was accompanied by the imprisonment of Lula Da Silva through a corrupt judicial proceeding, and the murder of feminist and lesbian social leader and Rio de Janeiro city councilor Marielle Franco – all amplified by the electoral victory that brought an overtly racist, homophobic, and misogynistic leader such as Jair Bolsonaro to the presidency. But we should also mention the opacity of the judicial proceedings that led to the imprisonment of indigenous social leader Milagro Sala in the Jujuy Province of Argentina in 2016, and the systematic persecution of figures such as Cristina Fernández de Kirchner in Argentina and Rafael Correa in Ecuador as soon as their presidential terms had ended.[2] However, this judicialization and criminalization of politics has also crossed the border to countries not considered populist. We could point to the reactivation of far-right and guerrilla positions in Colombia – bordering an exhausted Venezuela – through the rejection of the peace referendum; the election of far-right leader Iván Duque; the resumption of the murder of social movement leaders; the judicial persecution of popular political leaders such as Gustavo Petro, Francia Márquez, and Ángela María Robledo; and the rearmament of guerrillas, faced with a lack of protection and the murder of demobilized ex-guerrillas.[3]

Winds have also shifted in Europe. At the same time that SYRIZA, Podemos, and La France Insoumise showed their limitations and came up against difficulties beginning in 2018, xenophobic and racist discourses were on the rise. Thus, strong electoral performances by the likes of Marine Le Pen in France in 2017 and governments of Viktor Orbán in Hungary and Recep Tayyip Erdoğan in Turkey were joined by Matteo Salvini in Italy and the emergence of the Vox party in Spain. All of these represent agendas seeking, on the one hand, to roll back the collective accomplishments of feminism, of black, indigenous, and LGBTI+ communities and, on the other, to uphold traditional values like the family, property, and the irresponsible exploitation of nature. To this, we must also add Donald Trump's victory in the United States and his resolute determination to embrace this same agenda, to once again intervene in Latin American politics, to humiliate the European Union, and to declare a trade war on China. Although these examples do not exhaust the ways in which various reactionary or borderline reactionary positions have gained ground globally, they serve to illustrate the context in which our work and our theoretical–political concerns have unfolded. In any case, and in parallel to these advances by the right, we have also seen the victory of Alberto Fernández in Argentina; the reactivation of the progressive wing of the Citizens' Revolution in Ecuador; the persistence of Humane Colombia's pact for life, peace, and the environment; the consolidation of women like Alexandria Ocasio-Cortez in the United States and Francia Márquez in Colombia; the silent success of the Portuguese government and the pact between Podemos and the Spanish Socialist Workers' Party (PSOE) in Europe; the victory of Andrés Manuel López Obrador in Mexico; and the regional consolidation of a powerful popular feminist movement known as Not One Less.

Now, the current global scenario that we just described demands that we take up a series of questions not contemplated in classical debates on populist theory. We refer to debates on the opposition between left-wing and right-wing populisms and their relationship with neo-fascism, the emancipatory nature (or lack thereof) of populist projects, their ability to provide a true and lasting alternative to neoliberalism, the link between populism and institutions from the perspective of a popular and emancipatory state, the intersection between populism and plebeian republicanism, the potential for international populist solidarity, and, above all, the need for a fruitful dialogue between populism and popular feminist movements that are confronting patriarchal forms of power, property, and collective sacrifice. Toward this end, we found it much more suggestive to write seven theses on populism – each addressing a specific problem or position – rather than attempting to establish a unified and free-standing corpus. So the reader is not obligated to follow a specific reading order but can instead approach each of the theses independently, according to a web of concrete problems in each case. This is, therefore, an open book, whose subterranean connections between different sections, far from being exhausted by a unitary reading, make room for the uncertainty that each problem poses and the hope that the reader will be able to connect these problems according to their particular interests.

On the other hand, we should note that this book is also the result of a process of collective experience and organization. We could perhaps say that it has been weaving together ever since those initial investigations into populism that we each undertook alongside other researchers, leading to the publication of a groundbreaking book about Kirchnerist populism,[4] a study of the relationship between populism and republicanism,[5] and its incorporation into contemporary philosophical, political, and historical debates from different contexts.[6] But, above all, we must mention that this militant project would not have been possible without the field of study opened up by Ernesto Laclau's epistemic turn and later contributions by Chantal Mouffe and Jorge Alemán. Nor would it have been possible without the establishment of spaces such as the Ernesto Laclau Open Seminar at the Faculty of Philosophy and Letters of the University of Buenos Aires (UBA), the various projects and open discussion spaces at FLACSO-Ecuador, and the Theorising Transnational Populist Politics project funded by the British Academy.[7]

All of these spaces not only allowed the two of us to think together, but also brought together an extraordinary group of colleagues from different continents, both from the politically engaged academic community and from political life. Among them, we would like to thank Sofía Argüello, Javier Balsa, Luis Blengino, Ricardo Camargo Brito, Manuel Canelas, Germán Cano, Volkan Çıdam, Valeria Coronel, Mark Devenney, Allan Dreyer-Hansen, José Enrique Emma López, Íñigo Errejón, José Figueroa, Jorge Foa Torres, Javier Franzé, Zeynep Gambetti, Adoración Guamán, Julio Guanche, Gustavo Guille, Jenny Gunnarsson-Payne, Griselda Gutiérrez, Emma Ingala, María Cecilia Ipar, Andy Knott, Jorge Lago, Anthony Leaker, Juan Pablo Lichtmajer, Oliver Marchart, Sammuele Mazzolini, Emilia Palonen, Gloria Perelló, German Primera Villamizar, Clara Ramas, Franklin

Ramírez, Eduardo Rinesi, Anayra Santory, Ian Sinclair, Yannis Stavrakakis, Soledad Stoessel, Ailynn Torres Santana, José Luis Villacañas, and Clare Woodford, among others. These are the kinds of friends that politics and the academy give you when you share concerns, convictions, and the same way of understanding the importance of ethical-political commitment in all knowledge production. Likewise, we cannot fail to mention our infinite debt to Judith Butler, Penelope Deutscher, and their working group for having invited us to form part of the International Consortium of Critical Theory Programs,[8] one of the few truly democratizing consortia genuinely concerned with establishing an egalitarian, solidaristic, and fruitful dialogue between knowledge production in the Global South and in the Global North. And within this Consortium, we would particularly like to thank Rosaura Martínez Ruíz, Gisela Catanzaro, Natalia Brizuela, and Leticia Sabsay for having suggested, reviewed, and unconditionally supported the writing of this book. But there are four names that we cannot avoid repeating and to whom we owe particular thanks for generously reading and contributing to this volume: Gloria Perelló, Valeria Coronel, Juan Cárdenas, and Luis Blengino. So, while we wrote this book between March and December of 2019, we can say that the gestation of this work in time and space far exceeds the momentary frenzy in which it was written, and which involved working jointly at a distance, texts shared by email, opinions transferred through WhatsApp messages, discussions carried out through voice memos, and long virtual conversations between Bogotá and Buenos Aires.

Finally, we would like to point out that the title we have chosen for this book is not insignificant, but instead represents a nod to the irreverent creativity and heterodoxy of Latin American critical thinking, a tradition of which we feel we are a part, if only through the humble evocation of José Carlos Mariátegui's illuminating *Seven Interpretive Essays on Peruvian Reality*.

Bogotá and Buenos Aires, December 2019

Essay 1
The Secret of Populism

The returns of populism

"Populism" is an insistent word, one that returns to us every time we try to store it away in the chest (*arcón*) of disused terms in the political lexicon. As we know, a chest can serve as a coffin or a jewelry box; it can bury a corpse or guard a treasure. Or perhaps it can be both things at once, and what dies is capable of guarding a secret to be deciphered in our present. Let's not forget that the etymology of *arcón* is related to the arcane, meaning a secret or a mystery, i.e. something that remains closed and hidden. We could ask ourselves what it is about populism that remains hidden, or the secret of why it returns to the field of politics every time its death is announced. We might even wonder why there is so much interest in declaring its death and what the unspoken fear is that hides away its existence. As the word itself indicates, populism expresses a tendency or movement toward the popular, an adjective indicating that which refers to the people. So populism, as the storage chest of the political, holds the secret of the people. And perhaps that is the secret of its strength and its condemnation – perhaps that's why it divides the social field and lays bare antagonistic struggle through the establishment of a frontier between those on top and those on the bottom. If populism returns, if populism persists despite attempts to lock it away and make it disappear, this is most likely because those on the bottom resist domination by those on top, because those on top never cease to perpetuate mechanisms for the dispossession and exclusion of those on the bottom. Perhaps populism is the chest that those on the bottom store within their bodies and their memory every time they have the opportunity to contest the oligarchic meaning of the republic, because, in the end, populism can be understood as the way in which plebeians fight for the *res publica*, that public thing that oligarchies want to preserve as a treasure for themselves.

That's why, when the Washington Consensus[1] overwhelmingly shrank the terrain of political intervention in the late 1990s and early 2000s, the populist secret made a comeback in Latin America. Of course, this was initially considered an isolated anachronism, or merely an atavistic vice specific to peripheral countries and without broader global significance. But the rapid spread of populist governments across much of Latin America, and the subsequent appearance of populist leaders, movements, and governments in Europe and the United States, have again granted the term a prominent role in public debates and international discussion forums on the inter-regional level. In this context, the proliferation of political formations characterized as populist since the beginning of the twenty-first century has led different authors – even those with political positions as different as Chantal Mouffe (2018) and Éric Fassin (2018b) – to argue that we are experiencing a "populist moment." While these authors limit their analyis to the case of Western Europe, we can clearly also extend such a diagnosis to other latitudes. It only takes a brief review of the present or the recent past for an entire list of political experiences characterized as populist to come to light quickly. If, by the "populist moment" in Western Europe, we include the most well-known cases such as DiEM25, SYRIZA, and Golden Dawn in Greece, Podemos and Vox in Spain, Jeremy Corbyn, Boris Johnson, and Nigel Farage in England, Marine Le Pen and Jean-Luc Mélenchon's La France Insoumise in France, Matteo Salvini and the Five Star Movement in Italy, we could also refer to cases like Sweden Democrats led by Jimmie Åkesson, Víktor Orbán in Hungary, Jarosław Kaczyński in Poland, Vladimir Putin in Russia, Recep Tayyip Erdoğan in Turkey, and Rodrigo Duterte in the Philippines. And if we move over to the Americas, in the North we find Andrés Manuel López Obrador in Mexico and Donald Trump and Bernie Sanders in the United States; in South America, we have many examples, including the governments of Nicolás Maduro in Venezuela, Jair Bolsonaro in Brazil, and the recent administrations of Evo Morales in Bolivia, Lula Da Silva and Dilma Rousseff also in Brazil, Rafael Correa in Ecuador, and Néstor Kirchner and Cristina Fernández de Kirchner in Argentina, among others.

Moreover, if we look retrospectively and extend our inquiry to approximately the last 100 years of political life on a global scale, we can see that this "populist moment" was preceded by at least two others. We can locate a first "populist moment" in the mid-to-late nineteenth century, a period marked by the Russian Narodniki agrarian movement and the People's Party of rural movements in the southern USA, both traditionally considered to be pioneering examples of populism. We can locate the second populist moment in the period marked by the great movements that emerged in Latin America in the mid twentieth century (whose most paradigmatic cases, although not the only ones, were Varguism in Brazil, Peronism in Argentina, and Cardenism in Mexico). But, if we pay close attention to the intervals between these two moments, we can also find various political experiences that were classified as populist. For example, the astonishingly succesful Boulangist movement in France, the cases of early Ibañism in Chile, Yrigoyenism in Argentina, the Fort Copacabana revolt and the Prestes Column in Brazil (antecedents of Getulio Vargas' Estado Novo), and Kemalism in Turkey. We could also add the Revolutionary Nationalist Movement in Bolivia, Velasquism in Ecuador, Gaitanism in Colombia, Nasserism in Egypt, the experience of Tito in Yugoslavia, and Mao Tse-Tung's "Long March" in China. We could even include the cases of

Juan Velasco Alvarado in Peru and Muammar al-Gaddafi in Libya.

This whole enumeration of moments and experiences that have been classified as populist allows us to see that these have included both right-wing and left-wing formations, peasant and urban movements, and liberal-democratic, socialist, and authoritarian political regimes in the so-called "core" or "developed countries" as well as in the "periphery" or "developing countries." It seems as though this heterogeneous list could be extended indefinitely in an endless dissemination of examples, with moments marked by a greater concentration of cases. Perhaps we should, therefore, ask ourselves whether it is useful to continue thinking about populism simply in terms of "populist moments," or whether we need instead another sort of distinction that will help us better grasp that secret of populism that seems to spread across different geographies and historical moments. Along these lines, defining populism turns out to be difficult, given the variety and breadth of cases falling under that name, and this task only becomes more difficult given the well-known prejudice and disdain with which the subject is treated in the literature. If anything has thrown the debate on populism into the fray, it is its pervasively negative charge. Populism is immediately associated with the aesthetically ugly, the morally evil, a lack of civic culture, contempt for institutions, demagoguery, and irrationality. It has been described as a perversion or a pathology, accused of always containing proto-fascism, of being a fraud, a hoax, or a deviation. But in order to better differentiate between the various levels on which this disdain toward populism functions, we need to distinguish between three perspectives regarding its use: mediatic, empirical, and ontological.

We speak of a mediatic perspective because, at present, the word "populism" is usually used uncritically to group together all political experiences that don't fit within the model of liberal market democracy. So much so that, in 2016, the Foundation of Urgent Spanish – sponsored by the news agency EFE and BBVA bank – declared "populism" to be the word of the year (Martín, 2016). But the problem with this usage is that it encourages us to form a knee-jerk common sense that is more interested in generating immediate aversion to those processes deemed populist than in understanding the specificity of the phenomenon. It generates a series of confusions around the word's use that unfortunately permeate academia and hinder efforts to understand the different evolutions of populism and the rationality specific to it. With regard to this use of populism, then, we need to distinguish between the mediatically constructed spontaneous and pejorative dimension and the situational strength of populism as an experience that transcends the classic aspects and spatialities of populism.

The empirical perspective, in turn, sets out from the practical study of concrete political experiences characterized by: (a) a break with oligarchic and elitist states; (b) a very specific type of modernity; and (c) a linkage between the popular and state power (Germani, 2019). One characteristic of this kind of approach is that, despite focusing on the strictly empirical dimension of populism, it has led to a series of prejudices that conditioned its findings regarding populist experiences. Regardless of the author in question, the common denominator is the assumption that populism represents an unsatisfactory deviation. The particularity of this approach, then, is that populism never acquires the status of a political concept capable of serving as an explanatory paradigm – instead becoming an unsatisfactory response to a purported European model delineating the horizon of progress for any kind of democracy.

It was not until Ernesto Laclau's intervention, in his famous text "Toward a Theory of Populism" (Laclau, 1977), that "historical studies of populism" became a "general theory of populism" (Laclau, 2005a). This meant, on the one hand, abandoning the assumption that populism represents a failed historical form in peripheral countries and, on the other hand, understanding populism as a political logic that coincides with a form of radical democracy (Laclau and Mouffe, 1985) – in other words, to grant populism the dignity of a theory and to turn it into a political ontology for theorizing political articulations in general (Laclau, 2005a). Thus, and without wanting to simplify things, we can say that it is Laclau who introduces the ontological approach to populism, thanks to the astuteness of taking a term traditionally used to explain Latin American backwardness and elevating it into a form of political thought. Far from considering populism an imperfection, Laclau instead wondered if it wasn't time to stop comparing ourselves to supposed models – of which populism could only be a lesser copy – and begin to theoretically build the *logic of populism itself*.

Modernization, class struggle, and the constitutive dimension of the political

In this essay, we are going to set aside the mediatic perspective and focus on the tensions between the empirical and ontological approaches to populism. This will help us better understand, on the one hand, the different lines of inquiry in play around the populist question, and, on the other, how this transition from strictly empirical studies to the ontological plane took place. For us, the lines of inquiry along which the question of populism is theorized include: the problem of modernization in Latin America, the viability of the class struggle, and the constitutive dimension of the political. The first includes those works emerging from the general framework offered by modernization theory and comparative politics, predominant in the United States after the end of the Second World War. Standing out among these is the pioneering work of the Italian-Argentine Gino Germani (1968 [1956]), who understood populism as an anomalous path for transitioning from a traditional or "backward" society to a modern one. In other words, he linked populism to a specific phase of social development in modernizing countries. Through an analysis of the case of Argentina in the 1930s and 1940s – i.e. Peronism – Germani argued that the process of rapid industrialization and urbanization had created masses that were available for political action, and whose "early" intervention into politics disrupted the proper transition toward modernization, and thereby also eroded the institutionally appropriate forms of liberal democracy. He thus considered populist experiences to be the expression of an irrational relic preventing Latin American countries from following the path of European or American models of social change (i.e. a process of increasing social differentiation, specialization, and complexity, alongside a working class politicized through the organization of liberal political parties). All this led Germani to characterize populism as a phenomenon outside and hostile to representative democracy, which necessarily gave rise to authoritarian personalities.

Years later, Torcuato Di Tella (1965), a disciple of Germani, would analyze the populist aspect of Peronism in terms of the establishment of a relationship between "displaced elites" and "available masses." The "displaced elites" (composed of intellectuals not belonging to the working class, and who instead originated in different social sectors such as the army, the clergy, sectors of the bourgeoisie, or lower-middle-class professionals) had a social status that did not correspond to their expectations. Meanwhile, the "available masses" (comprising peasants and urban workers) were easy to lead insofar as they were dazzled by access to the city, public schools, and the media. Thus, the "available masses" – eager to participate in politics and achieve upward social mobility – joined forces with the "displaced elites" to give shape to populism, defined as a political movement with significant popular support in which non-working-class elites with an anti-status-quo ideology also participated.

If Germani and Di Tella's sociological approach turned populism into an anomaly that, of course, should be avoided, or at least corrected, this was due precisely to the fact that their works took on the perspective and categorical frameworks of mid-twentieth-century modernization theory and comparative politics. In other words, they studied populism according to a series of external criteria and assessments with serious limitations when it came to understanding specific logics produced from the Global South. These frameworks were based on the assumption that there existed a predominant pattern for modern society, toward which those societies characterized as traditional or backward should aspire and assimilate, bit by bit. This was therefore a hierarchical assimilation, since it was based on the idea that the Global North represented the only possible model for modernity, while simultaneously accepting its purported economic, political, and cultural superiority. From this perspective, modern societies were identified with the United States and Europe and were characterized as secular, adaptable to rapid change, cosmopolitan, and with a complex division of labor and a working class whose political culture was linked to liberal-democratic parties. Meanwhile, traditional societies were identified with Latin America, Asia, and Africa, and were described as religious – or even superstitious – conservative, closed, passive, economically and socially simple, and lacking a civic culture that would enable the development of liberal democracy. The only valid and possible way to achieve true modernity was to follow the trajectory of modern societies.[2]

Years later, Bertrand Badie and Guy Hermet (1993), despite their efforts to renovate comparative politics, did not manage to avoid the prejudices through which populist strategies had been traditionally analyzed. They argued that populist strategies, located historically and geographically in South America and Mexico – and to a lesser degree in mid-twentieth-century Asia and North Africa – "result from the reinterpretation of clientelist appeals with a plebiscitary, statist, and almost always dictatorial perspective" (1990: 203).[3] To arrive at this conclusion, they distinguished populism from both fascism and the "European Bonapartist phenomenon," insisting that what sets the former apart is "lower support from the middle classes and the internal orientation of its nationalism," as well as "an exaltation of the plebeian that Bonapartism only expresses with prudence or reticence" (1990: 202). At the same time, they allowed themselves to reproduce a series of stereotypes about those countries they understood as traditional, to the point of affirming, in the case of Latin America, things like the following: (a) the predominance of a system of large landholdings (*latifundios*) that makes clientelism a "nearly consubstantial" element of these societies; (b) that populism develops in a "context of clear state weakness ... and the oligarchic privatization of power"; and (c) that "the runaway urbanism affecting Latin American countries since 1918 and Near Eastern countries since 1951 is not, as it was in Europe, the result of industrialization" (1990: 202). These affirmations allowed them, in turn, to conclude that Latin America would not be ready for a true social transformation, and, by extension, that populism is an imposture blocking such transformation. More than anything, this is because the populist strategy consists of "pampering and privileging that small group of workers so that it does not fall into the temptation of revolutionary radicalism while at the same time reinvigorating the system of domination that guarantees what is most essential, i.e., the stability of traditional control in rural areas" (1990: 203). We could say that the most current contributions to this updated trajectory in sociology and political science are those of Carlos de la Torre (2000) who, in addition to reiterating prejudices about populism, adds the element of a populist technocracy, anchored above all in the experience of the Rafael Correa government (2013).

We could say that the second line of enquiry – research on populism from the perspective of class conflict – has woven together diagnoses that share at least one element with the first group described above (see Rinesi and Muraca, 2010; Cadahia, 2017).[4] The classic position, which emerges above all from a more orthodox Marxist tradition, argues that populism is the expression of a cross-class alliance that did not conform to the expected parameters of the class struggle. Populism was thus considered a kind of double deviation from an expected pattern. On the one hand, because the working class lost sight of its own fundamental and historically assigned task – the anti-capitalist struggle – and, on the other, because the workers diluted their role as social agents of their class into a diffuse entity like "the people." Albeit with different nuances, this argument runs throughout those traditional class analyses according to which populism was indistinguishable from Bonapartism[5] or inseparable from fascism, the latter being especially prevalent in works focused on the cases of Italy in the 1920s and Germany in the 1930s.

Subsequently, Miguel Murmis and Juan Carlos Portantiero (1971), proponents of democratic socialism in Latin America, presented a more sophisticated reading and argued that populism, far from betraying a sort of irrationality or delirium among the working class, was instead an expression of its pragmatism. While they assumed that populism represented a hegemonic project not of the working class, but of small business owners and the state bureaucracy, they recognized that it allowed the working class to make a series of demands about the distribution of income and the extension of their rights along multiple parameters. In some sense, this was a question of the dialogue between populism and socialism that defined the context for certain debates in Latin America in the 1980s. In the classic text "The National-Popular and Actually Existing Populisms," Portantiero and Emilio de Ípola sought to determine the central arguments according to which populism was considered antithetical to socialism, explicitly distancing themselves from Laclau and establishing a series of dichotomous divisions between both traditions. They therefore identified populism as a homogeneous, hierarchical, and statist movement, and socialism as pluralistic, horizontal, and democratic (De Ípola and Portantiero, 1981), but the central point of their argument was that populism was not a deviation, but a betrayal, of the popular cause. This was based on the idea that the crisis of oligarchic states in Latin America in the first half of the twentieth century had created the conditions for a truly plebeian national-popular movement to emerge and transform society, but populism was responsible for absorbing these national-popular forces and even transforming them into national-statist forces tied to capitalism. It was this confluence with the state and capitalism that prevented these authors from embracing the emancipatory dimension of populism that Laclau was upholding at the time (De Ípola and Portantiero, 1981).

Along similar lines – albeit several years later and without being aware of the work of these authors – Slavoj Žižek would again take up the Marxist critique of populism, this time filtered through psychoanalysis (2009). But instead of focusing on the dangers of the state capturing the national-popular, Žižek emphasizes populism's supposedly proto-fascist tendency, which externalizes the constitutive fracture of the subject onto an other. In this sense, the people of populism is always a "unified people" insofar as it needs an enemy to antagonize. In any case, Žižek returns to the traditional elements of the Marxist criticism of populism by once again associating it with fascism, and painting it as a hoax that distances the working class from its own definitive historical objective: to destroy the capitalist system.

On this point, we could say that, if there's one thing that modernization theory, comparative politics, and classical Marxism have in common, it is that they all understand populism as a deviation to be eradicated, albeit with one subtle but important difference. While the two first traditions assume that populism is a form of political organization that threatens individual liberty, the division of powers, and parliamentary democracy (De la Torre, 2013; De la Torre and Peruzzotti, 2008), the third, by contrast, understands populist practices as capturing emancipatory popular forces, subjecting them to the game of state power, and containing them within the logic of capitalism (De Ípola and Portantiero, 1981).

Now, it is within the third line of enquiry – the constitutive dimension of the political – that the pejorative interpretation of populism begins to be undermined and the foundations will be laid to think about its ontological dimension,[6] i.e. to what extent populism becomes a logic constitutive of the political itself – not a deviation from it – and how this logic articulates material forms of social being. On the one hand, we could mention those authors who have worked through the relationship between populism and democracy, and two fundamental works in particular – those of Peter Worsley (1969) and Margaret Canovan (1999) – that introduced the novelty of not seeing populism as a threat to democracy or as some kind of deviation. For Worsley, populism showed how representative democracy had reduced participation to a merely formal matter, and, consequently, rescued the value of participation over institutional procedures. In this sense, he believed that the properly populist relationship between the leader and the people refers to a general idea of participation that should not be considered an authoritarian defect a priori, without taking into account the context of its emergence. Canovan, for her part, reinforced this argument when she insisted that populism is a constitutive dimension of democracy that emerges in the ineradicable gap that every liberal democratic regime has between its two faces: the redemptive and the pragmatic. It is also merely a form that implies an appeal to the people against the dominant power structures, the content of which will depend on the context in which it is mobilized.

On the other hand, there are those authors who have interrogated the relationship between populism and republicanism – i.e., those who link populism to the republican tradition. Here we could cite the work of Eduardo Rinesi (2015), who believes that populism "is not only conflict and the crisis of all instituted powers, but also closure, hegemony, order, institutionality" (2015: 91). Moreover, Rinesi assumes that, even if he were to choose to accentuate (like Laclau) populism's antagonistic element, this would not nullify his thesis regarding the relationship between populism and republicanism, since there is a long tradition that emphasizes the conflictual and ruptural dimension of the republic. Because the *res publica* is always conflictual at some point, populism and republicanism maintain a complex bond of co-belonging where they cultivate shared elements (institutionalism and rupturism). Hence, we must reject the belief that populism is merely "the other" of institutions that it will always threaten. The positions of Valeria Coronel and Luciana Cadahia (2018) move along these same lines, highlighting the importance of exploring what types of institutions populism generates, without losing sight of, on the one hand, the fact that it aims to build a state that can account for the irruption of the popular masses into politics, and, on the other, its intrinsically democratic dimension, insofar as "populism is one of the few political experiences that keeps the figure of an empowered people alive" (2018: 77). It is along these lines that Coronel and Cadahia find the argument allowing them to support the same political thesis as Laclau – namely, that populism can acquire an emancipatory dimension.

In turn, we find debates about whether populism is a strictly emancipatory experience or whether, to the contrary, it is necessary to distinguish between left-wing and right-wing populisms. Among those who defend the distinction is Mouffe (2018), who proposes the construction of a left-wing populism as a valid political strategy for Western European democracies. Her main interest is to show how this strategy would open up the possibility of expanding democracy (by defending equality and popular sovereignty, constitutive elements of any democracy) in the context of a crisis of neoliberal hegemony and the emergence of authoritarian and anti-democratic right-wing populisms. Against this distinction, we find the thoughts of Jorge Alemán (2014, 2016, 2019), for whom this distinction makes no sense, and who instead reclaims the deeply emancipatory nature of populist legacies. It is within these debates about the constitutive dimension of the political that the ontological question of populism will emerge, allowing us to lay out the central thesis of this essay.

Populism as ontology of the political

Once we have reconstructed the most significant traditions and problems through which populism has been theorized from the Global South, we can return to the question posed at the beginning of this essay: should we continue to speak in terms of a populist moment with left-wing and right-wing strategies, assuming that populism is a sort of malleable form capable of adapting to very different political projects? Or would it be more advisable to delve more deeply into the idea that populism is not susceptible to just any kind of politics? Along these lines, it would be one thing to study populism as a merely conjunctural strategy – which is totally legitimate in terms of militancy – and another thing entirely to approach the conjuncture through its ontological dimension.

As we all know, it was Laclau (2005a, 2005b) who introduced the discussion in these terms, and the importance of his

work on populism can be summarized in how he managed
to grant populism the status of a political category in its
own right. Moreover, this achievement was framed within a
broader objective that, according to Laclau himself, constituted "a unique project: reclaiming the political initiative,
which from my theoretical perspective means making politics
thinkable again" (Laclau, 2008: 12). Thus, it was not simply
about reclaiming a historically stigmatized term, but about
showing us how – thanks to this term – politics could become
thinkable once more. Indeed, Laclau's entire theoretical
development since kicking off the post-Marxist approach
alongside Chantal Mouffe in *Hegemony and Socialist Strategy*
(1985) can be read in this sense. His proposal for a discourse
analysis of the theory of hegemony and antagonism that he
began to elaborate with Mouffe, his reformulation of the
concepts of reactivation and sedimentation, his later notions
of dislocation, heterogeneity, people, and leader can all be
understood within the same double movement: in both an
ontological and political key. In the first case, it can be read
as an attempt to return politics to its fundamental position,
and, in the second, as an insistence on the political effort
to operationalize emancipation. It should be emphasized
that populism acquires a fundamental position through this
double movement and becomes "a way of constructing the
political" (2005a: xi).

Without exhausting the complexity of Laclau's approach,
we could say that his conception of populism involved taking
up a Latin American debate and tying it to a series of concepts
from other traditions in order to shape his view of the
political. This meant theorizing populism through two logics:
the logic of difference and the logic of equivalence. Although
both are embedded within every social structure, Laclau
sought to privilege the logic of equivalence in populism. If
differential logic is characterized by segmenting demands and
satisfying them one-by-one, equivalential logic, by contrast,
begins to articulate different demands with one another
until achieving an equivalential chain capable of challenging
the status quo and establishing a frontier between those on
the bottom (the articulated people) and those on top (the

status quo). It is this frontier that shapes the antagonism of the social, an antagonism that is no less than the symbolic articulation of a condition of exclusion (Retamozo and Stoessel, 2014). Or, in the terms laid out at the beginning of this essay, it is the clarification of the conflict through which those on the bottom reveal themselves in the face of exclusion and dispossession by those on top. Thus, equivalential logic – because the demands are experienced as an unsatisfiable lack – organizes a hegemonic relationship overdetermined by an empty signifier that is identified either with one of the demands or with the figure of a leader. The other crucial aspect is that, for Laclau, this way of building hegemony around an empty signifier and through an equivalential chain can be taken up as a democratic project – i.e. as a way to radicalize democracy in terms of a hegemonic project for social equality.

Now, this belief that populism can be simply identified with the political provoked angry debates, even among those academics trained at the Essex School of Discourse Analysis that Laclau founded. Benjamín Arditi (2003, 2005) has argued that Laclau's theory was redundant and lacked conceptual specificity, since he deployed three semantically overlapping terms – hegemony, politics, and populism – which has only brought more confusion to the concept of populism. Oliver Marchart (2018), on the other hand, has pointed out that Laclau's best argument was precisely that populism is not simply another political expression that, after adequate conceptual clarification, can be added to the list of political formations: "Because populism is not simply a form of politics among others. In encapsulating political rationality *tout court*, it enables us to catch a glimpse of the nature of the political. Populism is the clearest expression of the logic of antagonism, which, in turn, is the defining feature of the political" (Marchart, 2018: 23).

Thus, if populism is the political form that responds directly to "the logic of antagonism," it turns out to be its fundamental form, since, for Marchart, antagonism is the very name of the political insofar as it is precisely its defining feature. In other texts, Biglieri and Guille (Biglieri, 2007;

Biglieri and Guille, 2017) similarly reject the idea of a mere semantic overlap and pose the idea of the mutual *contamination* of the terms constituting the antagonism. While this is close to Marchart's position, there is an important difference: the antagonism must be constructed politically in order to gain existence. In other words: we need a symbolic-imaginary construction that takes it into account, so we cannot simply speak, as Marchart does, of a "logic of antagonism," since antagonism only exists through its effects on hegemony and the logics constituting it (equivalence and difference). In other words, there is a hegemonic way of "doing" politics through antagonism, without which the latter would have no way of being expressed.

With regard to our argument, we pick up on the role of antagonism and the mutual contamination of populism and politics, which allows us to argue that every populist articulation necessarily implies a hegemonic articulation and, as such, is traversed by logics of equivalence and difference that generate frontier effects in the acting out of some antagonism.[7] These two logics – which cannot be joined together in a coherently unified way – and their border effects, are constitutive of politics and populism, hence their mutual contamination. Thus, once we have introduced the notion of contamination, we know that this cancels out the possibility of delimiting conceptual areas in a pure and pristine way. But it is still possible to establish certain features of the concept of populism that we will be working with in the following essays, namely: (a) the experience of a lack; (b) the inscription of that lack as a demand; (c) the primacy of the logic of equivalence over the logic of difference, giving rise to the subjectivity called the "people" (the *plebs* that claims to be the only legitimate *populus* – i.e., that part claiming representation of the whole); (d) the antagonistic dichotomization of social space into two overdetermined loci of enunciation – the people versus the enemies of the people; and (e) the emergence of a leader.

The main consequence of all this is that we can no longer think of politics as immune to the emergence of populism, and much less strive for its definitive elimination. Populism contaminates politics, is inscribed in politics itself, and thereby also in the people and its leaders. In any case, we can either have non-populist hegemonic articulations that are established on the basis of a variety of antagonisms, in the absence of a decisive leader naming a people – or we can have political formations that privilege the logic of difference and an institutionalized absorption of demands. But we should not lose sight of the fact that there is always the possibility that the multiplicity of antagonisms, at some point, becomes simplified around two chains of equivalence (the people versus their enemies) dichotomously dividing the social space.

So, once we grasp the idea that populism draws upon those elements that are the very condition of politics, we can see why Laclau argued that the populist gesture is "the royal road to understanding something about the ontological constitution of the political as such" (2005a: 67). It is feasible to say that a particular political articulation can be disarticulated, a specific people and its leader can be defeated politically, but populism as an ontology of the political is ineradicable. That is, in an ontic sense, and as an articulation linked to a specific form of political expression in a specific context, populism can come to an end, but, in a fundamental sense, linked to the very ontology of politics, populism is simply ineliminable.

Thus, Laclau's entire goal in "making politics thinkable again" was directly tied to his effort to rescue populism from the marginal and stigmatized place to which it had been relegated. Rescuing populism also means rescuing politics, because contempt for the former necessarily involved a biased and reductionist reading of the latter. De-stigmatizing populism within the theoretical field means simultaneously transforming the way the ontological dimension of the political is understood. It is therefore no longer a question of rescuing populism from the storage chest in which some want to lock it away, but rather of showing that populism is itself a chest that contains a series of secrets to be deciphered. And that meant, in the first place, deconstructing the contemptible place to which, according to Laclau, populism had been relegated by predominant approaches to philosophy and the social sciences. In Laclau's own words:

> Because of the suspicion, which I have had for a long time, that in the dismissal of populism far more is involved than the relegation of a peripheral set of phenomena to the margins of social explanation. What is involved in such a disdainful rejection is, I think, the dismissal of politics *tout court*, and the assertion that the management of community is the concern of an administrative power whose source of legitimacy is a proper knowledge of what a "good" community is. This has been, throughout the centuries, the discourse of "political philosophy," first instituted by Plato. "Populism" was always linked to a dangerous excess, which puts the clear-cut moulds of a rational community into question. So my task, as I conceived it, was to bring to light the specific logics inherent in that excess, and to argue that, far from corresponding to marginal phenomena, they are inscribed in the actual working of *any* communitarian space. (Laclau, 2005a: x)

So, Laclau not only sought to bring together a series of political phenomena that had been relegated to the fringes of social explanation, but, moreover, revealed the epistemic violence of an entire tradition of thought that had turned political work and explanation into the privilege of "experts." Populism, as praxis, became a dangerous excess because it came to question and disrupt "the clear-cut moulds" of a certain kind of political philosophy. And this turn, therefore, involved studying populism from within, from its own organizational logics. All of which contributed to finding in populism a singular way of theorizing the being of the social. Hence the controversial statement by Laclau and Mouffe, in *Hegemony and Socialist Strategy*, that "society does not exist" (1985: 26). This statement brought many criticisms that, in our opinion, owed to a deep misunderstanding of what these authors were proposing within the field of political thought. By saying that society does not exist, they deactivated obsolete, positivist views of society and introduced into the social the idea of lack, i.e. the lack of being – or being as lack. This new way of reading the being of the social helps us understand that the political is nothing more than working through the constitutive negativity of that lack

– a way of working on the social through a logic articulating this constitutive lack. What political theories, currents, and traditions cannot tolerate is not the deviation that populism engenders, but the ontological indeterminacy into which it throws us. Thus, the secret of the constitutive uncertainty and indeterminacy of being that Laclau's populism reveals, and which is symbolized in the heart of the political field, can be read today as the unconfessed inverse of those who needed to declare its death. What many could not bear was precisely the paradoxical nature of political work that populism revealed – namely, the impossibility of the social as a condition of possibility for political praxis, a praxis far removed from rational procedure and normativity and closer to the plebeian forms through which Latin America has built the social from the political. The ontological dimension that Laclau opens up, then, frees us from the stigma associated with the "failed" character of Latin American politics, and offers us the possibility of discovering in that failure not a deviation to correct but an ontological indeterminacy to work through. And it is on the basis of this ontological opening of populism that we are going to take up the challenge of working through a series of key issues that Laclau left entirely unexplored, and that our present moment demands that we confront in all of their radicalism.

Essay 2
Neither Left nor Right: Populism without Apology

Populism, left and right?

In the previous essay, we argued that populism cannot be limited to a mere political strategy, but that it must be understood in its ineradicably ontological dimension. Once we assume that populism is constitutive of the ontological character of the political, it is no longer easy to simply continue to uphold the ontic distinction between left-wing and right-wing populisms. This distinction is only plausible if we see populism as merely a political strategy. For this reason, in this section we will explore in greater detail the difficulties of maintaining only the strategic dimension of populism, i.e. all that is lost by subjecting it to a merely conjunctural plane, and even more so when the conjuncture in question is that of Europe.

As we indicated in the first essay, one of the authors who works most rigorously on the distinction between left-wing and right-wing populisms is Chantal Mouffe. In her latest book, *For a Left Populism* (2018), Mouffe considers this distinction to be necessary due to the partisan nature of politics, i.e. the fact that every hegemonic link – constitutive of populism and politics – responds to a contingent and non-essentialist interaction among particularities contending for access to a structuring position. In this way, the ability of a particular social force – a particularity – to become hegemonic does not guarantee that force a definitive victory, and will always be partial, precarious, and negotiable.[1] It is therefore on the basis of this partisan nature of politics that Mouffe interprets the current Western European conjuncture as a return of the political in the guise of a "populist moment" that can turn either to the left or to the right. According to her diagnosis, and given the advantages that the right seems to have over the left in Europe, Mouffe considers it a priority for the left to embrace its populist dimension and begin to compete with the right over certain signifiers. Put differently, Mouffe thinks it is urgent to begin to interpellate those who vote for right-wing populisms, since, in the absence of an irreducible identitarian essentialism, those same voters could be summoned by a call from the left. The hypothesis underlying Mouffe's proposition is that the forms of exclusion propitiated by the post-political ethos of recent decades – i.e. the disaffection provoked by European social democracies in their retreat toward a supposedly apolitical center, far from the slogans of the left and right – diverted many social sectors affected by neoliberalism toward right-wing populism. Along these lines, the author adds that many demands articulated by right-wing populism cannot be absorbed by that same neoliberal system, and could even be understood as having a democratic character. So, if right-wing populism was able to break with the post-political ethos of European social democracy and open up an alternative that allowed them to win the votes of vast social sectors, now it is left-wing populism's turn to do the same in pursuit of an egalitarian social justice that provides a true alternative to neoliberalism.

Mouffe's partisan stance (according to which every particularity is drawn toward assuming a structuring universalist role) and her anti-essentialism (according to which no demand is inherently left-wing or right-wing) provide her starting point for theorizing the possibility of building right-wing or left-wing hegemonic articulations around the same signifiers (for example: homeland, state, people, anti-neoliberalism, etc.). Therefore, the political orientation of those elements (or, more precisely, of any element) depends on a broader political articulation. Thus, the wager of her latest book is to call for disarming right-wing populisms, snatching away the democratic demands that they articulate, and, above all, those elements (like the state, the homeland, etc.) that the right has appropriated and which function as their nodal points, to instead endow them with truly emancipatory meanings.

It is interesting to specify that the distinction between left-wing and right-wing populisms is one of Mouffe's original contributions. While Laclau argued that the political orientation a particular populism can acquire depends on the correlation of forces in a given context, he never claimed that this orientation should be based on the left/right distinction, nor did he establish the fundamental features for establishing a binary distinction in those terms. Mouffe, by contrast, when determining the content of her distinction, favors an ontic classification of populism. This is because, after diagnosing the return of the political in Western Europe in the form of a populist moment, she tells us that, while left-wing populism must reinforce a democratizing position that defends equality and social justice, right-wing populism defends authoritarian, racist, and xenophobic positions that are contrary to any egalitarian aspirations (Mouffe, 2018: 17–24). So, in the contest between right-wing and left-wing populisms, it is the very construction of a people that is at play, and what is at play in their orientation on the left or the right is the question of affects. Or, to put it another way, the type of people constructed will depend on the affects mobilized, with the possibility that some affects are oriented toward reactionary elements and others toward emancipatory elements. We should clarify, however, that Mouffe's idea of the left differs from classic categories of social class, and even focuses on the need to articulate a heterogeneity of demands that are not necessarily anchored in class categories.

So far, we have elaborated the main arguments Mouffe deploys to establish the strategic distinction between left and right populisms in Europe. It is true she is dealing with a very interesting conjunctural position that has generated many

European examples, including La France Insoumise under Jean-Luc Mélenchon, the progressive wing of the Labour Party under Jeremy Corbyn, and Podemos in Spain. But we also believe that this conjunctural position runs the risk of, on the one hand, neglecting the evolution of populist experiences in Latin America – where the right/left distinction has not interpellated us in the same way as in Europe – and, on the other hand, abandoning the ontological dimension of populism and the way the logic of the political is articulated.

If we stop to ask whether populism's logic of political articulation is (or is not) constitutively emancipatory, Mouffe's position would lead us to respond in the negative, since populism would operate as a mere form that is open to any type of content. But this would be negative not only for Mouffe, but also for most of the authors trained at the Essex School, many of whom agree with Mouffe's interpretation that populism can take on both right-wing and left-wing political orientations. Marchart, for example, takes this for granted when he states that 'other demands might change sides and become articulated with political forces and discourses of completely different, perhaps opposite provenance. This is what happened in the case of current right-wing forms of populism where demagogues of the political right effectively managed to integrate leftist demands for social security and the defence of the welfare state into their xenophobic discourse' (2018: 118).

For his part, Yannis Stavrakakis (2017) also accepts the flexibility of populist political orientations when he argues that:

> This perspective highlights the emancipatory potential of certain populist discourses in representing excluded groups and facilitating social incorporation and democratic representation against oppressive and unaccountable power structures. At the same time, it remains alert to the fact that, due to the irreducible *impurity* of every relation of representation, due to the sliding capacity of signification, even genuine popular grievances and demands can end-up being represented by illiberal and anti-democratic forces or becoming hostages of authoritarian institutional dynamics. (2017: 528–9)

So it becomes necessary to make explicit the divergent evolutions of populist theory in different loci of enunciation. If the left/right distinction seems unavoidable in the case of Europe, we need to ask why this is not the case for Latin America. Or perhaps to ask ourselves whether we can offer reflections on populism from the Latin American locus of enunciation that might disrupt some of those arguments constructed from Europe.

Is all populism right-wing?

Just as the authors mentioned above are suspicious of the constitutively emancipatory dimension of populism and reassert the left/right distinction, there are other authors like Éric Fassin (2018a, 2018b), Slavoj Žižek (2009), and Maurizio Lazzarato (2019) who reject the distinction but for reasons completely opposed to those we will discuss below. According to these authors, the left should not fall into the populist "temptation" because to do so would bring with it nothing but the worst right-wing authoritarian elements. These authors warn us that populism contains the fantasy of the "one-people" – the people understood as a self-enclosed identity, or a homogeneity that blocks the emergence of differences. Žižek believes this because, as we mentioned in the first essay, he connects populism directly to fascism, insofar as populism always needs "to be supplemented by the pseudo-concreteness of a figure that is selected as the enemy, the singular agent behind all the threats to the people" (2009: 280). From this point of view, populism displaces and unleashes the constitutive antagonism of the social onto a positive entity, which becomes the repository of frustrations to be eliminated, thereby preventing justice from prevailing within the people. The consequences are obvious for Žižek: populism always fails in the attempt. Populism is merciless toward an enemy or outsider that needs to be eliminated, thereby losing sight of the primordial battle that everyone on the left should be eager to fight: the fight against capitalism itself, rather than, for example, getting sidetracked by financial speculators.

For his part, Fassin warns us against the fascist seduction involved in populism's claim to embody the people in a "totalizing we," which would aim to dissolve minoritarian plurality into a popular unity (2018a: 9). Moreover, the author adds, populism is motivated by sad passions that have nothing to do with the passions motivating the left: a "great resentment" against minorities based on "the idea that there are others who are benefiting instead of me; if I am not benefiting it is their fault. And that same impotent rage becomes enjoyment ... of playing the victim" (2018a: 39). But it should be noted that the resentment Fassin speaks of is not that of the "losers of neoliberal globalization," as Mouffe (2018: 21) describes voters of the populist far right:

> but of those who, whatever their success or their failure, insist that others, who can't hold a candle to themselves, are doing better than they are. It is in these terms that we can understand the rage against minorities and women, but also against those on "benefits": right-wing populism detests nothing so much as the undeserving poor, those poor people who deserve nothing more than what they have, or rather who don't even deserve that. Or their rage against the fools of the left, those with degrees and the arrogance of not realizing that the cultural capital that benefits them only has value in their own eyes. In other words, those who have lost their courage without losing their pride. (Fassin, 2018a: 36–7)

In that sense, Fassin offers us an impoverished and reductionist reading of resentment, even displaying a contempt for popular sectors and a profound incapacity to feel empathy for the exclusion they suffer under neoliberalism. What's more, he considers that the resentment fostered by the one-people of populism can be (and is) compatible with neoliberalism. Thus, the author adds, populists' fundamental battle is against minorities, not against neoliberalism. The case of Trump is proof: his sexist, racist, and xenophobic populism guarantees "neoliberalism's popular success" (2018a: 25), and, regardless, his electorate has been defined primarily in terms of a (sexist, racist, and xenophobic) cultural battle, with little concern for Trump's economic policy.

In a paper entitled "From Pinochet to Bolsonaro and Back Again,"[2] Maurizio Lazzarato (2019) has diagnosed a new wave of fascism, racism, and sexism on a global scale (whose most recent episode is Bolsonaro's election in Brazil), directly connected to the birth of neoliberalism in Chile under the Pinochet government. In dealing with the Brazilian case, Lazzarato detects this connection between fascism and neoliberalism as having emerged through populism, which demonstrates the perversion he is trying to denounce. The populist government of Lula Da Silva and the Workers' Party (PT) was perverse to the extent that it was a great implementer of neoliberal policies under the banner of wealth distribution. On the one hand, it basically transformed the poor into debtors, since, by seeking to reduce poverty and improve the conditions of the working class and proletarians, it did little more than incorporate them into the financial mechanisms and financialization of their lifestyle. And, on the other hand, the Lula government reconfigured the state and its functions according to the basic terms of the neoliberal program: a strong state that guarantees the operation of the free market economy.

Lazzarato's political conclusion is that the application and subsequent failure of these policies led to the electoral victory of the fascist Bolsonaro, replicating the situation of the initial imposition of neoliberalism that, on a global scale, first occurred in Latin America. An accumulation of frustrations gave rise to the fascist temptation. Big capital's strategy in Brazil, threatened as it was by the 2008 financial crisis, was the same as in Chile in 1973: to reconfigure an alliance with large agricultural producers, businessmen, the military, and religious groups (Catholic priests in the case of Chile, evangelicals in Brazil), all of which gave rise to the fascist revanchism of elites and the white upper middle classes, whose class hatred toward President Lula (and, we could also add, Dilma Rousseff) was also fueled, among other things, by inclusive policies for black university students and labor regulations for domestic workers. To all this, according to Lazzarato, we should add the role played by the frustration of the poor and of workers, because a micro-credit policy like that implemented by the PT ended up creating the conditions for a micro-political fascism centered on the figure of the unsatisfied individual consumer. This was because, on the one hand, it configured indebted subjects, vulnerable to the fear and anguish of finding their everyday lives financialized, producing a depoliticizing individualism and a superficial consumerism that was insufficient to roll back an unequal social and productive structure. And, on the other hand, because it fueled the consumer logic of buying all kinds of durable goods (cellphones, televisions, etc.) at the expense of basic issues like access to drinking water, sewers, paving roads, or opening schools and hospitals. Thus, the massive demonstrations in 2013 against the Rousseff government were an expression of this frustration, anger, and disappointment with the PT project that cleared the way for fascism. In short, for Lazzarato, Lula's (and Rousseff's) populism bears the most blame for the rise of the fascist Bolsonaro.

At this point, we could pose a series of questions to all of these authors who reject the emancipatory possibilities of populism and identify it with the right, with neoliberalism, and with fascism. Regarding Žižek's position, one might ask whether it is possible to confront a political struggle against the "system as such" and avoid the antagonism that emerges when specific interests are threatened, forcing us to face concrete enemies. For example, is it possible to fight against financial capitalism – or capitalism as such – without antagonizing the flesh-and-blood financial speculators themselves? Is it possible to engage in a "universal struggle" without passing through a particular one? In some sense, to suggest that populism is entangled with a particular is to accuse populism of "positivizing" antagonism, since the positive moment occurs when I identify an adversary and constitute myself in opposition to them. Along these lines, Žižek suggests that such an operation would be an externalization of my own self-negativity, since I would be projecting onto the other a fracture or lack that is within myself. While it is clear that Žižek seeks to weaken populism by accusing it of positivizing the antagonism, we might ask ourselves how effective this strategy is. Is it not possible to assume that this form of positivization exists, and still continue to think that populism is necessary? When Žižek counterposes the figure of self-negativity as something prior to the struggle against an adversary, he is also setting out from a positivized way of theorizing antagonism – namely, my self-negativity. The fallacy of his argument is that it makes us believe that identifying the negative moment with the self-negativity of the subject is a way of "escaping" positivity and recuperating radical antagonism. The criticism that Žižek seems to aim at populism could also be applied to his own strategy.

It's one thing to say subjects trick themselves into believing that the eradication of the other would mean the consummation of their identity, and a different thing entirely to assume that their political identity – the type of identity we are discussing here – is constructed in relation to what it opposes: the adversary. If we pay attention to how actually existing political struggles work, Žižek's critique seems strange. When a social movement or collective takes to the streets, it does not believe that the accomplishment of a demand means the full realization of its identity. It simply needs this accomplishment in order to be able to realize a part of itself that has been denied. According to Žižek, our position would entail "the positivation of our negative relation to the other [the master]," while he believes that the real question has to do with the "positivation of our own ... negative relationship towards ourselves" (Žižek, 1990: 253). But is it not precisely in the experience of my negative relationship with the other that I find that I am something different from "myself?" We could say that it is in the experience of resistance that social fabric is built, that forms of articulation that escape the mere positivization of our negative relation to something are consolidated.

On the other hand, a political actor knows themselves by being other things at once, acting in other spheres where they need to solve other problems having to do with the constitution of their identity. Obviously, political struggle does not seek the "physical" elimination of the adversary, but rather the transformation of the position they occupy within a given relation of forces. And success means not only the dissolution of the adversary's position of power, but also of mine as well, since my position will also be transformed by the new situation. What is most disheartening about Žižek's strategy is that, according to the logic that the slave "yields to the desire of the master," we could reject any protest or collective grievance, since we could always resort to the argument that, in the face of discontent, the individuals in question are merely externalizing onto another – the master – their own lack, that negativity through which they feel something preventing them from being themselves. Would this imply that the history of class struggles – within which Žižek claims to position himself – has been nothing but yielding to the desire of the master? In the final instance, we could say that the experience of my own flaw is translatable through an outside understood as a set of biographical, historical, traumatic, and collective sedimentations that are reactivated within me to cope with this constitutive flaw, with politics being the way of externalizing the flaw and working through it – no longer through a solitary "self-satisfying" withdrawal, but instead through collective, plebeian praxis.

As far as Fassin's position is concerned, he seems to reproduce a sort of essentialism and a fixation insofar as he anchors a series of passions in the fascist/populist right from which the left would seem to be exempt. Are there passions that are exclusive to the right, and others exclusive to the left? Do resentment and rage only suit the right, and does indignation only suit the left? If we effectively maintain that "resentment does not turn into rebellion, just as indignation does not turn into bitterness" (Fassin, 2018a: 39), we risk falling into the *naïveté* of believing that the left is always noble, always good, and incapable of harboring sad passions in its heart. To do so would be to reproduce those purist clichés that Mouffe herself sought to question by proposing the indeterminacy of signifiers and the partisan nature of politics. As we have said above, even if signifiers like the homeland or the nation are sedimented within right-wing discourse in Western Europe, nothing prevents them from being reactivated at a certain moment and under specific circumstances, and contested by political positions with other ideological orientations.

Finally, and with regard to Lazzarato's position, we believe it is fair to ask: if it is true, as he argues, that populism is a fraud clothed in wealth redistribution, while in reality facilitating neoliberal policies, then why have neoliberal elites devoted all their effort and wealth to combating and displacing populist governments not only from Brazil, but from Latin America as a whole? Why have neoliberal elites unleashed persecution against populist leaders once they have left office? Curiously, Lazzarato cites the case of Lula as a paradigmatic example of populist deception: is he aware that Lula has been jailed under an absolutely dubious judicial proceeding typical of the logic of "lawfare?"[3] Does he know that something similar is happening in Argentina with Cristina Fernández de Kirchner, or in Ecuador with Rafael Correa – both also subject to judicial proceedings that lack due process? Why are neoliberal elites – now that these populist leaders have left government – doing everything they can to prevent them from returning to political power? Perhaps lodged within Lazzarato's text is a set of prejudices among the enlightened left toward the material importance of populism for popular sectors. Lazzarato is alarmed that Lula's populism favors consumption by the poor before managing to meet their needs for health centers, schools, sewers, and drinking water, as if this were still more proof that populism is a scam that does not aim to resolve the true needs of the dispossessed. But, without minimizing the importance of public policy in providing basic services to the community, why should the possibility of popular sectors accessing durable goods always be deferred? Is access to consumption not a social achievement?

As Latin American intellectuals, we find it very problematic every time a European intellectual – who enjoys guaranteed access to consumption – questions those experiences through which broad popular masses have the opportunity to access levels of consumption that neoliberalism denies them over and over again. Why does a Parisian intellectual know better than those most excluded themselves how they should rationally rank their own priorities, what kind of goods they should have access to, and where they should circulate given the position they occupy within the social order? This is why, so often, we hear scandalized complaints about how populist leaders simply gain the support of those most excluded by fraudulently promising a level of consumption that is not appropriate to them, as if this was either a vote of fools who allow themselves to be tricked or irrational people who don't know how to vote for the good of the community. As if the educated sectors or the middle class *do* know! It seems then that what is truly scandalous and unacceptable to some enlightened elites is for the popular classes to *enjoy* themselves.

Paradoxically, this critique is compatible with the neoliberal critique of populism in one aspect. Suffice to mention statements by two senior officials from the neoliberal government of Mauricio Macri in Argentina, who, after the departure of the Kirchner government in 2015, followed the same sort of reasoning as Lazzarato.[4] One example was that of Javier González Fraga, appointed President of the Bank of the Nation, who came to argue that: "You made an average employee believe that their average salary was enough to buy cellphones, plasma-screen TVs, cars, motorcycles, and to take trips abroad. That was an illusion. That was not normal."[5] The other comes from Vice-President Gabriela Michetti, who said that "The most difficult thing for us is to get through the moment when you leave populism and leave the fantasy of an important and enormous lie – telling people that they would be able to live this way forever because we have the resources for that."[6] Therefore, the concern we want to raise here points at the heart of a certain tradition of leftist thinking that, as we saw in the example of Lazzarato, makes arguments that end up being secretly complicit with the right-wing sensibility in the region.

Just populism

So far, we have critically developed the arguments of those who either appeal to the distinction between right-wing

and left-wing populisms or reject this distinction to support
the idea that all populism is inherently right-wing. It then
remains for us to think through what populism might mean
without the stigmas associated with the right and with
authoritarianism. Along these lines, we find thinkers like
Jorge Alemán (2016), who, like Žižek, thinks through the
lens of Lacanian psychoanalysis and takes a relatively critical
position toward Laclau's work. Alemán agrees with Laclau
when he argues that populism is the alternative to neoliberalism, but distances himself from Laclau when he argues
that neoliberalism does not respond to hegemonic logic.
To support this second statement, he turns to the notion
of capitalist discourse developed by Jacques Lacan.[7] The
peculiarity of capitalist discourse, Alemán tells us, is that it
functions as a "counter-discourse" that seeks to appear to
itself without any internal division and seeks to eliminate
the possibility of imagining anything outside of itself. In
turn, it promotes two movements that are, at first sight,
contradictory: it closes inward on itself – in the sense that it
continues its repetition and elimination of differences – and it
expands limitlessly by closing off any idea of an outside. This
is to such a degree that Alemán even suggests that capitalist
discourse functions as a commodity that attempts to cover
completely the entire symbolic universe. And this action is
possible, Alemán adds, because it attacks precisely what is
proper to the subject – namely, its constitutive flaw, the flaw
that functions as the condition of possibility for the subject to
exist through it. This is how capitalist discourse blocks constitutive dislocation and prevents the irruption of the subject.
Or, put another way, what the Argentinean thinker is trying
to tell us is that capitalist discourse is configured in such a
way that it prevents the irruption of anything other than its
own reproduction. In turn, this characteristic of capitalist
discourse allows Alemán to account for the functioning
of neoliberalism in the present, since it behaves like "an
acephalic force which expands limitlessly until the last limit
of life. This is precisely the novelty of neoliberalism: the
capacity to produce new subjectivities configured according
to a corporate, managerial, and competitive paradigm of

existence itself" (Alemán, 2016: 15). So, while neoliberalism presents itself as a rationality in search of maximum freedom that seeks to promote a diversity of subjectivities, what it brings about is the opposite: the oppression of blocking the constitutive flaw in the structure, of avoiding any interruption, and of nullifying differences. Its incessant repetition always brings us back to the same place in the unlimited circuit of commodities.

On the other hand, Alemán also warns us that the most sinister aspect of neoliberalism is that it is the first regime in history that tries to unify two different dimensions of the symbolic order of language. It seeks to crush together into a single plane both the structural-ontological dimension of language with respect to the constitution of the subject (through which the living being is captured by language and turned into a subject even before being born and after death) and the socio-historical dimension of any order (the contingent discursive configurations of every period). While these two dimensions (ontological and socio-historical) appear as mixed, they follow different logics. The first implies an ineliminable dependency, whereas the second is a socio-historical construct susceptible to transformation. In this sense, the specificity of neoliberalism lies in this attempt to "accomplish the first symbolic dependence, affecting both bodies and the capture by the word of the living being in its structural dependency" (Alemán, 2016: 14). It seeks ultimately to unify the socio-historical with the ontological and to suppress the latter – i.e. to suppress the constitutive flaw or dislocation on which we depend on the ontological level, and which functions as condition of possibility for the socio-historical level. The great danger of neoliberalism, then, is its attempt to colonize the ontological dimension from which neoliberalism itself – as a socio-historical formation – emerged, and all to prevent socio-historical alternatives to capitalist discourse from emerging on the ontological level. If neoliberalism were to accomplish this unification, Alemán tells us, it would have consummated the most perfect of crimes, in the sense that structural dependence – the symbolic identification that allows the subject to be part of a transgenerational chain – would be devastated. In short, whereas structural dependence is the condition of possibility for shared historical legacies, the neoliberal regime attempts to "produce a 'new man' made from its own present, unclaimed by any symbolic cause or legacy, and which is as precarious, 'liquid,' fluid, and volatile as the commodity itself" (Alemán, 2016: 14).

Having arrived at this point, Alemán agrees with Laclau, since any attempt to block constitutive lack (or what Laclau calls dislocation) is a commitment to totalization. The only difference is that, while Laclau theorizes this lack within the very being of the social, Alemán instead locates it in the subject. But what is clear is that, for both, any attempt to block that lack, whether on the order of the subject or the order of the social, is a totalizing movement. And the reason for this is very simple: because differences can only exist thanks to this constitutive lack. So, filling this lack (or dislocation) means blocking the differences and hetero-geneity that constitute us as subjects or social beings. And any attempt at totalization brings only oppression, because any effort to annul dislocation is an attempt to block "the source of freedom" (Laclau, 1990: 76).[8] If this structural gap is considered a source of freedom, it is because it contains no structural determinations for the subject (hence it is the source of freedom and, therefore, the moment of decision beyond structure). By contrast, capitalist discourse, in its neoliberal modality, proposes to make the subject's experience impossible by contiguously connecting every place and reducing every difference to its commodity circuit. Thus, faced with this limitless neoliberal circuit with no possible interruption, Alemán, like Laclau, argues that hegemony – and particularly its populist version – limits that circuit, or at least seeks to install a circuit-breaker that would allow the establishment of border effects through the articulation of elements that never nullify difference and that assume the "impossibility of society." Further, hegemony rejects neolib-eralism's totalizing efforts by functioning as an arrangement that tolerates the flaw, that allows the irruption of the subject and the emergence of subjectivities that escape the totalizing emplacement of neoliberalism. This is why neoliberalism hates hegemonic articulations and any thought of emancipation (Alemán, 2016: 17–19). Consequently, populism:

> is not a renunciation of the radicalism of revolutionary transformation, it is more radical still, because in a materialist way it admits the impasses and impossibilities that appear when the part that is excluded and unrepresented by the system seeks to establish itself as a hegemonic alternative to the dominant power ... The people [*El pueblo*] begins when the category "people [*gente*]" is revealed to be a purely biopolitical construct. Meanwhile, the *pueblo* is as strange and singular as the subject itself in its mortal, sexed, and speaking becoming. The *pueblo* is an unstable equivalence constituted by differences that never unify or represent the whole. However, the fragility and contingency of its origin is the only thing that saves it from television, experts, programmers, accounting, etc. But it is only from within the most intimate folds of the mechanisms of neoliberal domination that the popular subject can arrive. (Alemán, 2016: 21)

If we follow Alemán's words rigorously, the people of populism is not a unity understood as a self-enclosed identity that expels differences. On the contrary, this people is possible thanks to its constitutive heterogeneity and the possibility of expressing itself through differences that are (equivalentially) articulated in an unstable way. Thus, it is possible to conclude that the people built through populism is diametrically opposed to the totalizing one-people that Fassin, Žižek, and Lazzarato accuse it of being. Furthermore, this people is not configured as a negation of the constitutive flaw, but thanks to it, such that this way of building the flawed and limited identity of the people can only be emancipatory.

Populism without apology

It seems that at this point we confront a dilemma that requires us to make a decision. In the case of Mouffe, Marchart, and Stavrakakis, it seems that two types of people can be built through populism: one authoritarian and exclusionary, the other emancipatory and egalitarian. In the case of Fassin, Žižek, and Lazzarato, on the other hand, populism always builds the kind of one-people that any leftist project should avoid. And, finally, Alemán suggests that the people of populism is constitutively emancipatory. Let's try to delve a little deeper into the first position, since our concern is the following: does the construction of two different types of people take place within populism, or should we theorize this tension along other axes? Along these lines, the question that we wish to ask, and which has not been explored so far, is whether the kind of people built by what this first position would call right-wing populism is not instead fascism. In this sense, it is possible that the return of the political of which Mouffe speaks should perhaps be understood not as a populist moment, but instead as a tension between populism and fascism, as two different ways of building the people and mobilizing shared affects.

Now, we think that, in order to move forward with this concern and to try to find a satisfactory answer, it becomes urgent to approach it through the question of equality. Mouffe tells us that right-wing populisms "do not address the demand for equality and they construct a 'people' that excludes numerous categories, usually immigrants, seen as a threat to the identity and prosperity of the nation" (2018: 24). In other words, equality is no concern for the populist right, but only for those left-wing populisms that make equality their defining feature, since there is an axis between equality and inclusion that makes a populism democratic, that leads it to work in pursuit of social justice, and that ultimately defines it as being on the left. Coronel and Cadahia (2018) also take equality as a necessary attribute for populism to acquire an emancipatory political orientation and avoid the reactionary dimension of the popular. They emphasize that we build this equality as long as we direct our antagonism against "those on top" and not against "those alongside us" – i.e. when a hegemonic link is produced through an articulation among those on the bottom that allows them to build antagonism against those on top. Coronel and Cadahia call this type of hegemonic relation common to all emancipatory populism a "plebeian link" (Coronel and Cadahia, 2018: 77–8).

Like these authors, Stavrakakis tries to theorize the specificity of this egalitarian hegemonic link, finding that it emerges when the dichotomization of social space occurs vertically (those on top / those on the bottom, high/low), which distinguishes it from exclusionary populisms that dichotomize social space horizontally (insiders/outsiders). The latter is what is usually referred to as far-right (or exclusionary) populism, which is, according to the author, the product of xenophobic nationalist ideologies with "only peripheral and/or secondary populist elements" (2017: 530). For Stavrakakis, exclusionary populisms can only possess secondarily populist elements because, while the people functions as a fluid empty signifier in inclusive populism, in exclusionary populism "the people" refers back to a transcendental, spectral signified, like the nation or the race. We would, thus, be in the presence of what Derrideans call "transcendental signifieds" – i.e. reference points that seek to fix meaning once and for all (Stavrakakis, 2017: 530). Thus, Stavrakakis, who takes the distinction between inclusionary and exclusionary populisms from Cas Mudde and Cristóbal Rovira Kaltwasser (2013), after filtering it through Laclau and Mouffe's discourse analysis, warns us that it is essential to distinguish populisms from nationalisms – giving the latter a pejorative and identitarian charge:

> In populist discourses *proper*, then, apart from being located at the core of the discursive articulation, "the people" operates as an empty signifier, as a *signifier without signified*, so to speak. ... In this sense, whereas (predominantly inclusionary) populist discourses potentially expand the chain of significations associated with "the people" – even including immigrants – (predominantly exclusionary) nationalist uses of "the people" attempt to arrest and limit this fluidity. ... At the same time, in spatial terms, populism *proper* is structured around a vertical, down/up or high/low axis that refers to power, status and hierarchical socio-cultural positioning ..., while nationalist or national-populist discourses prioritize a horizontal arrangement fashioned along the lines of nationalist out-grouping. (Stavrakakis, 2017: 530)

At this point, we would like to return to the concern with which we began this section, namely: if there is such a thing as populism "proper," then why continue to refer to derivative formations – i.e. so-called "exclusionary populism," "right-wing populism," or "nationalist populism" – as populism at all? Unlike Mouffe, we argue that, from the perspective of its constitutive structure, all populism – if we follow Laclau's (2005a) argument – is traversed and shaped by an egalitarian logic insofar as it privileges a logic of equivalence, i.e. a logic that articulates different demands that become equivalent with one another without being eliminated. We know from Laclau that the people is the political subjectivity of populism, and that the possibility of a people emerging depends on, among other things, the existence of "equivalence relations hegemonically represented through empty signifiers" (2005a: 156). And, from his work with Mouffe (Laclau and Mouffe, 1985), we also know that chains of equivalence are articulated not because the particularities constituting them have a shared goal, but because the elements involved are defined negatively, i.e. as differences. Their particular demands are extremely diverse, but nevertheless their claims become equivalent to one another vis-à-vis those excluded. In any case, if we can say that two or more elements become equivalent to one another – that is, they become equal – it is because they are different from each other. In Mouffe's own words: "a relation of equivalence is not one in which all differences collapse into identity but in which differences are still active" (2018: 63).

The question then inevitably arises: where does the difference between the left and the right lie if both respond to a privileging of equivalential logic insofar as they establish a people? Our argument is that the distinction lies in how they treat equality – i.e. how they manage differences and how they organize these vis-à-vis equivalence. While the populism we have called emancipatory organizes differences through articulation – meaning that it doesn't suppress the constitutive heterogeneity of those differences – right-wing populism instead organizes these through homogeneity. We could say, then, that right-wing populism seeks to impose equality through a uniform and dominant standard that eliminates constitutive heterogeneity in favor of uniform homogeneity – the one-people – since from this perspective notions of equality and difference are incompatible with one another. This is why equality is confused with the identitarian through the homogenization of differences among those who are part of the people, a dynamic that Georges Bataille described as follows in "The Psychological Structure of Fascism" (1985 [1933]: 137–8): "Homogeneity signifies here the commensurability of elements and the awareness of this commensurability: human relations are sustained by a reduction to fixed rules based on the consciousness of the possible identity of delineable persons and situations; in principle, all violence is excluded from this course of existence."

In other words, it is about the aspiration to eliminate differences from "those alongside us," accommodating them within a decoded space in order to establish a social configuration that is full, completely occupied, flat, transparent, and, ergo, free of potholes, flaws, fissures, antagonisms, or heterogeneities, in which the fantasy of the one-people can finally circulate. This fantasy may seek to establish itself on the basis of various elements (race, nation, religion, heteronormativity, etc.), but, in any case, it involves the violence of trying to dissolve the play of difference–equivalence into a broader identity. A self-transparent people. This is the fantasy of the one-people that contains the longing for a life without problems or antagonisms within the tranquility of a homogeneous social space, where all differences are located in a fully legible space, in pursuit of an equality posed in identitarian terms. If this way of constructing the people is not capable of "tolerating" the constitutive differences of the articulatory logic of populism, should we continue to call it populism, especially when the classic term "fascism" exists? How could it be both ontologically and strategically correct to conflate fascism with a populist form of popular construction? Along these lines, it therefore seems much more radical for us to defend the position that the identitarian logic of what has been called "right-wing populism" is in reality a reactivation of fascism, in Europe and Latin America alike. For populism, unlike fascism, equality does not entail any attempt to eliminate differences through homogenization. Quite to the contrary, populism supports and sustains differences insofar as it is established on the basis of the constitutive antagonisms of any social space and built upon the articulation of the most diverse heterogeneities, playing with the always irresolvable tension between particularism and universalism, difference and equivalence. In any case, the delineating of the antagonistic border against "those on top" encodes the desire that it not always be the same people who die: the poor, the plebeians, minorities, "the disposable ones" as they are called in Colombia, and the "little black heads" and "the shirtless" in Argentina. And it indicates an alertness to the fact, moreover, that someone else can always link up with this extensive chain of equivalent differences.

Wouldn't "right-wing" populisms fit directly under the label of fascism – or, more precisely, neo-fascism or post-fascism – inasmuch as they attempt to homogenize differences, and moreover have shown their ability to conveniently establish an alliance with neoliberalism? If the answer is yes, then the distinction between "left-wing" and "right-wing" populism or "inclusionary" and "exclusionary" populism loses its meaning. Let's just use "populism" as a synonym for left-wing populisms or inclusionary populisms without having to apologize, without having to clarify with adjectives. We will leave the rest for neo-fascism or post-fascism, i.e. a political formation characterized not by the nostalgic, point-by-point emulation of the fascist experiences of the 1920s and 1930s, but which has the particularity of combining an identitarian and immunitarian logic with neoliberalism.[9] Thus, the list of political formations named as populist in the previous essay can be narrowed down. Neither Trump nor Le Pen, nor Farage, nor Vox, nor the Golden Dawn, nor Orbán, nor Erdoğan, nor Bolsonaro are populists. The only label that fits them is neoliberal fascism. But the debate around neoliberalism remains to be tackled in the next essay.

Essay 3

Against Neoliberal Fascism: From Sacrificial Identity to Egalitarian Singularity

Is populism a form of neoliberalism?

One of the arguments used by populism's detractors, like Žižek (2009) and Fassin (2018a), to insist that populism is right-wing is the belief that there is a perverse link between populism and neoliberalism. This claim has opened up a very interesting debate between those who argue that populism represents a continuity of neoliberalism, and those who argue the opposite – namely, that populism can be understood as an alternative to neoliberalism. Those of us who take up the second position know that there are two questions at play in these debates that need to be developed in greater depth: on the one hand, to show that populism is not neoliberal, and, on the other, to explain populism's emancipatory wager.

In the previous essays, we formulated two important assertions about populism that we would like to take up again, since they will help guide our reflections on the link between populism and neoliberalism. In the first essay, we assumed that populism could not be reduced to a political moment or strategy, and that it had to be grasped in its ontological dimension – i.e. as constitutive of the political. This allowed us to delve more deeply into the type of articulation of the political that it gives rise to, and the way that difference and identity function when configuring the people. In the second essay, we explained all the difficulties associated with the difference between left and right populism. We distanced ourselves from this distinction and showed that the logic of political articulation of so-called "right-wing populism" does not function in the same way as the political articulation of "left-wing populism." While the former configures the unity of the people through a mechanism of identitarian exclusion – by showing that an external element threatens identity – the latter, on the other hand, builds upon articulations that tolerate difference. In other words, when configuring the people, there is a very important difference between a reactionary identity that seeks to expel those elements that threaten that self-enclosed unity, and an identity embraced as something to be built on the basis of constitutive difference and its ontological indeterminacy. That's why, once these distinctions have been elaborated, we prefer to replace the term "right-wing populism" with "fascism," and even to insist that the debates around left and right do not help us to discover the ontology of populism. So that what goes by the name of left-wing populism we'd rather just call populism, plain and simple.

Having made these clarifications, we are in a better position to explain why populism can function as an alternative to neoliberalism. Toward that end, in this essay we begin by collecting arguments from different currents of thought that maintain the belief that there is a perverse linkage between the two, and explaining why we consider this interpretation to be wrong. In particular, we build upon arguments formulated by parts of the European democratic left, Latin American autonomist thought, and republican democratic philosophy in Latin America and Spain. With these critiques collected, we will introduce arguments for why we consider populism an emancipatory alternative to neoliberalism, which in turn will imply clarifying how we understand neoliberalism and why it differs from populism.

The prejudices of the liberal, anti-communist left

With regard to the first current, which poses a link between populism and neoliberalism, we would like to return to and explore a little bit more arguments that we have already mentioned, by the French sociologist Éric Fassin in his book, whose Spanish edition (2018a) was titled *Left-Wing Populism and Neoliberalism* (original French title: *Populisme: le grand ressentiment*). The argument of his book is very simple, as we have mentioned in previous essays, focusing more than anything on the European setting and arguing for the need to reactivate a democratic left that keeps its distance from populism. Fassin believes that the democracy for sexual and ethnic minorities that he hopes to promote from the left could be threatened by populism's idea of the people. For him, populism confuses democracy with a unitary image of the people – the one-people – that dissolves the multiple dimensions of minorities into a restrictive popular unity. He even goes so far as to believe that the danger of populism is that the logic of majorities could come to overshadow minorities, understood as the only ones capable of changing how we understand the people and turning it into a plural and democratic public. This is why he prefers to abandon the idea of a people and, instead, to speak in terms of publics, which would allow us to avoid becoming trapped within an image of the people as the representation of a given reality, and to embrace it as a plural and diverse construct. He therefore concludes that what is at stake as an alternative to neoliberalism for the left is not the people but democracy, and that this should be promoted by an agenda to the left of the populist left.

Engaging in politics through the people is something that Fassin leaves to right-wing populism, assuming that the left has nothing to do with the people, above all because the people identified with right-wing populism cannot be reappropriated by the left. The pessimistic thesis that presumes the immobility of people's political perceptions

– as if human beings fall "naturally" to the right or the left – is problematic, but this is precisely Fassin's starting point for theorizing the link between neoliberalism and populism. He begins by saying that populism was born in response to the crisis of social democratic neoliberalism, but that, as a result, it does not offer any alternative. In this regard, he proposes the thesis that populism's anti-elitism is not necessarily opposed to neoliberalism, but to develop this argument he focuses on what he considers right-wing populism. Taking Trump's link to his electoral base as his example, Fassin attempts to show that this relationship does not emerge through a rejection of neoliberalism, but through shared xenophobic and racist values. And, in turn, the image of Trump as a successful businessman who knows how to maneuver in a competitive world is key to the success with which his voters identify. So the people that Trumpean populism alludes to is not that of the multitude, but of white men with neoliberal values.

The first thing we could say here is that Fassin excludes from his argument any reflection on why what he calls left-wing populism is also neoliberal, thereby leaving his argument truncated and limited to the experiences of the right. He only faintly alludes to the fact that left-wing populism would not be an effective weapon against neoliberalism because "repatriating populism to the left will not bring the desired electoral results" (Fassin, 2018a: 39). This quote shows something very problematic, since right-wing populism is assumed to be prior to its left-wing variant, as if the left had to convince a racist, xenophobic, and neoliberal people of something different. The other drawback of this interpretation is that it leaves aside the form of articulating the political that we maintain throughout this book – namely, that populism assumes neither a preordained identity nor a mechanism of identitarian exclusion. That's why we insist that what Fassin understands as right-wing populism we would call fascism. By giving his argument this twist, we can only say that Fassin invites us to think that fascism is related to neoliberalism, but he would not have anything to tell us about populism as we understand it in this book. Instead, he has left it entirely unanalyzed by reducing it to an unsuccessful electoral strategy.

Fassin leaves similarly unexplained the mechanisms by which people come to identify as fascist, xenophobic, or even patriarchal. The major difference between his argument and ours is that all of these identifications operate as the way people negotiate their dissatisfaction and constitutive lack.[1] In other words, we don't think that people are naturally xenophobic, racist, or patriarchal and seek to harm others – which would be an inverted romanticization of the people. On the contrary, we argue that all these exclusionary logics are a way of symbolizing the constitutive wound and flaw of the social, identifying this flaw itself with a hatred toward the other. And it is this understanding of the complexity of political subjects that allows us to understand that it is not so much a question of "changing the people," as Fassin suggests with a strangely elitist (and even unconfessedly anti-communist) wink – it is about changing *with* the people.

Autonomism: the opium of the people

From the perspective of certain representatives of Latin American autonomism, by contrast, the link between neoliberalism and populism is posed in different terms, and the emphasis placed on the role of progressive populist experiences in different countries in the region. If we turn to the theses of Maristella Svampa and Massimo Modonesi, in their co-authored article entitled "Post-progressivism and Emancipatory Horizons in Latin America" (2016), we see that they reject out of hand the idea that 21st-century populisms can be considered post-neoliberal. In this sense, they assume that the opposition between populism and neoliberalism is a false one that responds to a binary representation of reality, one that leaves out the role of social movements in emancipatory processes. By bringing in this third actor, the authors attempt, on the one hand, to break the link between populism and social movements – to the point of positioning them as antagonistic political forces

– and, on the other hand, to locate progressivism and neoliberalism on the same side. In other words, they consider social movements to be the only genuine and truly emancipatory force, and progressivism to be a unique neoliberal force, but one nevertheless aligned with capitalist dispossession. To support this argument, Svampa and Modonesi take the position that it was the social movements of the late 1990s that made possible a scenario of creative resistance and alternatives to neoliberalism. According to them, these types of plebeian struggles were anti-state and opposed to the logic of unions and political parties, and it was thanks to these struggles, they add, that progressive political parties were able to win elections and impose their new governing agenda. So these authors insist that plebeian irruptions were used, co-opted, and betrayed by progressivism's institutionalist and developmentalist agenda. We share with these authors the assertion that social movements helped set the stage for the emergence of progressive parties, but we would add that the consolidation of that force also depended on the acute crisis that neoliberalism was undergoing. All of which opened up a moment of reactivation that called into question the sedimented practices – and, with them, the legitimacy – of traditional parties, and the institutional arrangements of liberal democracy. Otherwise, we would not be able to understand why, in countries not considered populist (in Central America, Colombia and Peru, to name just two examples), social movements which did not experience this alleged co-optation by populism failed to articulate themselves as a force capable of defeating neoliberalism. It should also be noted that in many cases, social movements themselves invaded the state and began to create alternative institutional dynamics. In other words, it would be a mistake to establish a static dichotomy between social movements on the one hand and institutions on the other, as if there were no porous experiences through which they mutually contaminate one another. In this way, a synergy is created within the state between institutional logic and political militancy that transforms how the state operates and produces new "organizational logics" (Perelmiter, 2016).

This is why – here distancing ourselves from Svampa and Modonesi – we find it difficult to assume that the triumph of progressivism meant a betrayal of plebeian forces. We find it more accurate to think that, in reality, the triumph of populism has meant access for plebeian forces to the state as an inscription surface for emancipatory popular demands. Assuming that these forces are present only in social movements means completely neglecting the mode of political articulation of populist parties, their link with grass-roots organizations, and, above all, the plebeian origin of leaders like Evo Morales or Lula Da Silva who later became presidents. But let's weave these arguments more finely.

For Svampa and Modonesi, the plebeian irruption of the 1990s was characterized by the creation of new horizons for thinking about social relations and emancipation. While these were multiple, motley, and contradictory experiences, they were characterized by complaints against the stripping of fundamental rights, a profound questioning of party and union logics, and the attempt to formulate a demand for autonomy that would allow the socialization of power and the resignification of natural resources. This new "militant ethos" – as Svampa and Modonesi call it – made it possible to overcome the subaltern condition of the poor, to create a demand for emancipatory autonomy, and to build a new form of territoriality. Thus, the revolutionary socialist paradigm of the 1960s and 1970s was displaced by a new form of popular organization – one that rejected the logic of "seizing" state power. This questioning of classic modes of plebeian power, these authors insist, allowed for the creation of non-bureaucratic, horizontal, and democratic forms of plebeian social relations.

However, Svampa and Modonesi argue that the emergence of progressive governments perverted this entire process, to the point of transforming plebeian strength into populist power and emancipatory social transformation into a Caesarist passive revolution. Populism, therefore, represents a sort of decisionist power that disarticulated movements from below and extended the logic of neoliberalism in three key aspects. First, by continuing its developmentalist and extractivist agenda; second, because it was incapable of transforming the economic model or successfully combatting social inequalities; and third, because it returned to the statist logic that social movements had sought to distance themselves from. And this is the case for Svampa and Modonesi because the co-optation of the plebeian meant replacing a horizontal logic with the verticalism of the party, and replacing autonomy and self-determination with hegemony and statism, so that the only agenda social movements could have maintained in the face of populist governments was the demand for territoriality against neo-extractivism. Therefore, the authors conclude, it would be a mistake to try to defend progressive processes in the region – which ultimately represent a continuation of neoliberalism – and the task is instead to reactivate the new demands and organizational forms of social movements, and to propose an agenda that moves beyond 21st-century populism and contributes to the creation of a post-progressive and truly emancipatory scenario. The interesting thing about these criticisms is that, despite wanting to disassociate themselves from the revolutionary socialist paradigm of the 1960s and 1970s, they reiterate some of the classic socialist critiques of populism. Therefore, before reflecting on the authors' arguments, it seems important for us to show which aspects of those debates they reiterate.

We could say that the place autonomism assigns to social movements is equivalent to the place socialism assigns to the national-popular collective will. In the classic 1981 text by De Ípola and Portantiero, "The National-Popular and Actually Existing Populisms" – to which Svampa and Modonesi give a nod when they call one section of their article "the drifts of actually existing progressivisms" – the tensions between socialism and populism are sharply expressed.[2] In a very synthetic way, we could say that for De Ípola and Portantiero populism and socialism share the desire to build a hegemonic, national-popular project that provides an alternative to the nation-form of oligarchic states. Along these lines, and after the crisis of the oligarchic state-form in the early twentieth century, they add that populism had the opportunity to organize that plebeian national-popular force in order to consolidate a social transformation. But populists betrayed that possibility when they turned the national-popular into the national-statist, configuring a verticalist, homogeneous, and anti-democratic form of power, at the same time that they missed the opportunity provided by the crisis for a new recomposition of the state. If we look closely enough, Svampa and Modonesi are offering very similar arguments, since they also emphasize the recomposition of the state by progressive institutionality, and the betrayal of the plebeian irruption through Caesarist mechanisms.

If the populisms of the first half of the twentieth century were understood as a betrayal of the popular collective will, those of the early twenty-first century, from the autonomist perspective, represent a betrayal of social movements. Or, to put it differently, the plebeian transformation of social movements was reified by the populist form; the demand for autonomy subordinated by state interpellation; and the search for emancipation reduced to a decisionist, verticalist, and charismatic Caesarism or passive revolution. With these coordinates sketched out, the state is identified with oppression, verticalism, and de-democratization, while social movements are identified with emancipation, horizontality, and democracy. The question that can be asked here is why the expansion of rights that populism fosters cannot be read as a form of autonomy in terms of a people's own capacity for self-determination through the use of law, a form of autonomy that would contribute – even if formulated from above – to emancipation (the possibility for the self-realization of our capacities), horizontality (we all enjoy equal rights), and democratization (the expansion of popular power).

Does the fact that a measure is taken from above necessarily mean that it subalternizes plebeian sectors? Why is it that autonomists cannot understand social victories, often achieved through the articulation of the state and social movements – like the media and same-sex marriage laws in Argentina, the nationalization of water in Bolivia, or the regulation of domestic workers in Ecuador[3] – as steps toward self-determination and emancipation from particular forms of popular oppression (Stoessel, 2014)? Are these not the demands of social movements when they call for free university education or land regulation to avoid forced displacement? Are the interpellations of social movements not a way of demanding more institutionality, and the presence of the state in places that it has not historically reached?

If one of the peculiarities of neoliberalism is how it distorts the meaning of democracy and increases the distance between popular sectors and access to rights and institutions, it might be extremely useful to ask whether 21st-century populism has helped to reconfigure this link. It is clear that populism has often failed to live up to this synergy between popular demands and the expansion of rights, but making the link between these demands and the state the epitome of oppression will not help us advance one iota toward understanding actually existing forms of social emancipation, and much less the possibilities that this articulation opens up for continuing to radicalize democracy in our region. Perhaps more attention needs to be paid to the forms this return takes and the types of institutional displacement that each populist return produces throughout the course of Latin American history.

The argument for the "populist betrayal of the people" only makes sense if we set out from one premise: that the people and the state are two antagonistic and self-contained social products. If the state is assumed to be a sort of monolithic and self-contained power, an immutable universal form destined to oppress by its very nature, then it would make sense to think of the people as its antithesis. But if we instead understand it to be a porous and antagonistic social product in which different political forces strive to shape it and determine its institutional configuration and modes of accumulation and distribution, then it is more difficult to simply embrace this dichotomy without further ado. Is there not perhaps in this crisis and recomposition of the state the reiteration of a founding act of law exercised through popular desecration? In this sense, it is more interesting to reverse the question and wonder about the type of theological movement that authorizes us to imagine national being "liberated" from state "alienation" and recuperated by the "people." It is as if autonomism, through the unconfessed persistence of a sort of essentialist nostalgia, came to heal the communal wound caused by the emergence of the state. It could be said that this is the form of liberation that populism calls into question, since there is no such thing as a "national essence" that the "state" hijacks for private purposes, and nor is there such a thing as a people, given as a prior reality, awaiting liberation. If there is one thing that populism helps us to understand, it is that the state does not have to be a form of alienation, strictly speaking, but can instead become a way of articulating the popular. The confusion lies in believing that every form of articulation is a mode of alienation that oppresses a given materiality.

Here we see how the underlying problem is none other than the illusion of immediacy – i.e. the assumption that there is something unarticulated (or unmediated) that is stolen from the people, and that the key to emancipation lay in its spontaneous return. If the oligarchic state was the elitist expression of a particular state-form, that does not mean that every state-form is reducible to the same. It was the oligarchy that made the state the property of the few, so why not think that it might be the act of popular desecration that transforms institutions into a space for the nobodies to express their antagonisms. This is where we find populism's greatest innovation: to risk building a state-form that can account for the irruption of the people into politics. And we want to emphasize the word "risk" because, beyond the fact that it is impossible to translate fully the moment of popular irruption into an institutional arrangement, populism takes the risk of "working with" the antagonism that this irruption implies. That is why we wonder whether it is not possible to speak of a populist institutionality that coincides with neither the oligarchic state nor the European liberal-conservative state. And we believe that Latin American political thought today is still trapped in the impossibility of answering this question.

What we have done so far has been to deactivate the oppositional relation that autonomism poses between plebeian forces and progressivism, and between social movements and the state, so that it becomes possible to think of these as the same form of articulating the popular in two different instances, albeit not one that is without tensions, limitations, and contradictions. Therefore, to say that progressivism is an extension of neoliberalism is to completely overlook the way that populism articulates political subjects.

Now, there is one aspect that we have not yet mentioned and that is how the territorial demands of urban and peasant social movements have been processed. In this sense, Svampa and Modonesi's critiques of extractivism are completely accurate and expose very well one of the Gordian knots of contemporary populism, namely: thinking through a different relationship to nature. However, despite insisting that progressivism is neo-extractivist, these authors do not offer a satisfactory definition with which we could establish a debate.

Two other autonomist authors – in this case, Verónica Gago and Sandro Mezzadra, in their 2015 article "For a Critique of the Extractive Operations of Capital" – do offer an interesting definition, about which we could say a few words. First – and here differing from Svampa and Modonesi – they do not reduce the notion of extractivism to the operation of extracting raw materials, but rather extend it to other types of operations, like the extractive logic of algorithms in social networks, or a sort of "digital mining" whereby young people play for the accumulation of points or virtual goods that are then sold on the market. So, extractivism exists as much financially and digitally as it does in the extraction of inert materials and in the workforce, which, in addition to a sort of neoliberal governmentality, also implies a complex and heterogeneous form of social cooperation (Gago and Mezzadra, 2015: 43). By showing this complicity between the financial and the social, these authors attempt to slip in the hypothesis that Latin American populist governments have done nothing but encourage this form of extractive articulation.

From our perspective, and despite agreeing on many of the drawbacks of extractivism, it seems like a serious mistake to think that the populist form of articulation is identical to the extractive logic woven between the financial and the social. The point is that criticizing extractivist logic does not have to mean we must diametrically oppose populism, as Svampa, Gago, Modonesi, and Mezzadra seem to think. Isn't it more constructive to examine how populist logic could radicalize an alternative to neoliberal extractive logic and foster other kinds of subjectification? So, marking the limit of a political experience – an actually existing experience – should not lead us to automatically dismiss its ontological possibilities,[4] especially if that ontology, as we have shown in the first two essays, gives us the tools to formulate an alternative to neoliberal ontology.[5] We believe, as we have been insisting throughout this book, that there is a radical difference between populist forms of subjectification and neoliberal forms of subjection. To fail to recognize the role that the political plays in the construction of both subjectivities is to miss an opportunity to theorize an alternative through the very materiality of the existing. We believe that at the heart of the extractivist problem is the sacrificial logic that organizes and sustains it. So, as we will show toward the end of this essay, it is necessary to explore further what is at stake in sacrificial ontology, in order to better understand why populism does not reproduce it as a foundational structure of the political.

Populism as transitional object?

We now turn to the third theoretical tradition that seeks to establish a link between populism and neoliberalism. We refer to the proposals of a specific republican philosophical tradition interested in populism, which are expressed very rigorously by José Luis Villacañas in his book *Populism* (2015).[6] What is interesting about Villacañas' inquiries is that, unlike the other authors mentioned above, he proposes an ontological examination of populism, republicanism, and neoliberalism. Through a discussion of the link between populism and republicanism, he tells us that "Republicanism shares some aspects with populism, but above all it is an autonomous, ancient, and respectable political tradition, in relation to which populism represents an enormous simplification" (Villacañas, 2015: 119). This tension – but not opposition – that Villacañas establishes between the two traditions is due to the fact that "there would be great solidarity between neoliberalism, which destroys the very foundations of a socio-political republicanism centered on public institutions, and populism which attempts an urgent solution" (Villacañas, 2015: 119).

While this diagnosis is designed more for the European than the Latin American case – especially if we remember that populism has been one mode of building institutions in Latin America – the truth is that he poses a highly original connection between the two traditions. By considering populism to be a sort of "emergency brake" for neoliberalism, he merely makes clear the internal link to it, a connection that contemporary populist experiences have not been able to reflect on in all its radicalism and, as a result, they show signs of exhaustion today.[7] In this sense, Villacañas opens the door for us to start thinking about populism in its epochal dimension and to wonder about populism's temporalization – in a more philosophical than historicist register – based on its own contradictions and in connection to what it seeks to distance itself from. Thanks to this dimension opened by Villacañas, we can ask ourselves: why does populism fail, beyond its mode of articulating the political, to create an epochal common sense – or what Gramsci would call a historical bloc – that provides an alternative to neoliberalism?

But the author adds another important point in his book, a sort of constitutive ambiguity of populism, when he says that, just as populism is allied with neoliberalism, the same can be said of republicanism. There is, thus, a sort of virtuous link between populism and republicanism, understood as an alternative to neoliberalism. However, once he makes this suggestion, once he raises this epochal opening, the author chooses to understand this link in transitory terms, as if populism were that transitory experience, that necessary but disposable step that helps us take the leap towards a civic republicanism (Villacañas, 2015: 111–20). But, from the Latin American perspective, it is very difficult to understand populism as a merely transitory experience, especially if we understand it to be one of the few political experiences that has continued to expand the rights of the majority against the dispossession of rights by neoliberal institutionality. In other words, populism has functioned in Latin America as a form of plebeian republicanism, and so trying to think of it as a transitory device would mean neglecting how much populism has shaped our republics from a popular perspective.

Populism: antithesis of neoliberalism

So far we have done nothing more than to show how each of the currents mentioned above (liberal left, autonomist, and republican) have understood the link between populism and neoliberalism, but we have said little ourselves about how we understand the latter. So it becomes necessary to pause and think about what we are talking about when we use the word "neoliberalism." This exercise will help us explain much better why we think populism is not just another expression of neoliberalism, and that it even carries a secret alternative within itself. It should also be noted that, when we speak of neoliberalism, we mean it as an expression of capitalism – i.e. as an ethos configuring a specific way of life in the repro-duction of capital.

To expand upon these ideas, we will focus on Michel Foucault and Wendy Brown's research on neoliberalism, since they point in the direction that we are interested in exploring. In his classic text *The Birth of Biopolitics* (2010), Foucault defines neoliberalism as a practical response to the crisis of the art of liberal governance, which impacts two levels at the same time: forms of government and processes of subjectification. Regarding the first aspect, neoliberalism functions as a specific art of government, whose mode of acting is characterized by a transformation of state rationality in which the economy begins to be the creator of public law

(Foucault, 2010: 84). Foucault will establish a very important distinction between the statist, disciplinary rationality of modernity and the neoliberal rationality of government today (Foucault, 2010: 75–100). The main aspect that we hope to stress has to do with the role of the law in each type of practical rationality or governmental form. While, in the first case, law operated as an external limitation that provided a basis for determining what was prohibited and permitted within a government, in the second, an economic self-limitation arises from within the very practice of government that is accompanied by an "anti-statism, or state-phobia" (Foucault, 2010: 76). This will entail a transformation in forms of statehood, since the focal point is no longer a law or a right establishing what is forbidden and what is allowed, but instead comes to be located in consensus and practical interest (Foucault, 2010: 84–5). Thus, consensus, as a form of governmentality, displaces the legitimacy given by the law and begins to function as the new mechanism of state legitimation (Foucault, 2010: 84). The legitimacy of neoliberal states therefore does not depend on using law and institutions well in a republican sense, but on the ability to reach consensus and agreement on issues of economic interest. Although Foucault does not put it this way, we could say that the neoliberal state ceases to conceive of subjects as citizens with rights within a *res publica*, and begins to understand them instead as individuals with private interests in the market.

This new approach implies a transformation in the production of subjectivity, since Foucault tells us that the logic of free and self-interested profit-maximizing behavior extends to all spheres of human life. This is why, with regard to the second aspect, the immediate effect on processes of subjectification was the emergence of *Homo economicus* as the interface between this new form of governmentality and the individual (Foucault, 2010: 225–6). Foucault will show that, within neoliberal rationality, *Homo economicus* is not a partner in the exchange and consumption of commodities, so that the classic image of the individual consumer fails to reflect the historical mutation that this new rationality entails within individuals. On the contrary, this *Homo economicus*, as an individual who obeys their own self-interest, is an "entrepreneur of himself," a producer of capital through his own strength (Foucault, 2010: 215–33). And becoming an entrepreneur of oneself produces nothing but, as Brown suggests in her interpretation of Foucault, a vicious circle of obedience to one's own self-interest and the demand to produce infinite value in the reproduction of one's own life (Brown, 2017: 310).

Although Brown follows the lines set out by Foucault regarding neoliberalism, she will identify two major limitations that allow her to offer a more specific and complex elaboration of the phenomenon. First, she criticizes Foucault for understanding individual self-interest as the starting point for analyzing neoliberal practices. According to Brown, it is a mistake to think that self-interest "captures the ethos or subjectivity of the contemporary neoliberal subject," since hiding behind this statement is a certain essentialism that leads to the uncritical assumption that the nature of the individual consists of "self-interested actions" and that the expansion of this self-interest is the foundation of the neoliberal ethos (Brown, 2017: 83). Brown criticizes this belief because, for her, the figure of the individual – or the narrative around how *Homo economicus* functions – does not coincide with what really occurs in neoliberal practices. In this sense, the neoliberal individual "is so profoundly integrated into and hence subordinated to the supervening goal of macroeconomic growth that its own well-being is easily sacrificed to these larger purposes" (Brown, 2017: 83). In other words, to take the self-interest of *Homo economicus* as our starting point is to lose sight of the role that the economy and the state have in the construction of this figure, and the sacrificial dimension of this supposedly free choice. So what really takes place is a "governance of responsibilized citizens" that forces the individual to embrace their role as a "self-investor" and a "self-provider" at the service of the "health of the economy" and of "morality of the state" (Brown, 2017: 84). Thus, the belief that, in neoliberalism, each individual pursues and intensifies their private interest is one that "is made, not born, and operates in a context replete with risk, contingency, and potentially violent changes, from burst bubbles and capital or currency meltdowns to wholesale industry dissolution" (Brown, 2017: 84).

The second limitation that Brown identifies is that it is an error to believe that *Homo politicus* is simply displaced by *Homo economicus*. In this sense, she believes that Foucault lost sight of the political dimension and limited himself to the interaction between the individual and the market – or at best the heterogeneous dimension of the subject as both a legal and economic subject. She even criticizes him for having reduced the notion of sovereignty to the coercive role of the state and neglecting the idea of popular sovereignty configured during the French and American revolutions – namely, as something that is built and circulates between people (Brown, 2017: 86). In other words, Foucault focused too much on the individualizing role of neoliberalism and neglected the collective dimension of each of these aspects, and so Brown will pay attention to a double aspect neglected by Foucault. On the one hand, she is interested in the collective dimension of this new form of rationality – i.e. what happens to the *demos* of democracy, to the collective will, and to popular sovereignty in this whole process of the individual isolation of responsibility and the massification of these individual-izing effects. And, on the other, she is interested in studying the *Homo politicus* that survives and resists, thereby making possible alternative forms of subjectification and democracy.

Having reached this point, our goal is to rescue from Foucault and Brown the idea that neoliberalism is an epochal ethos organized around certain practices of government, and that these practices tend to organize a particular economistic link of the subject to itself and others, and between the state and citizens. However, we are going to steer clear of Foucault's characterization of *Homo economicus* and remain closer to Brown's clarifications, meaning that we are going to assume that *Homo economicus* as human capital, far from representing the expansion of private interest, instead represents individual sacrifice to the health of markets. And, in turn, we are going to pick up from Brown the idea that, despite the power of neoliberalism, there exists a *Homo politicus* fighting for alternative forms of subjectification and government beyond neoliberalism. Along these lines, and in the face of the neoliberal subjective emplacement given in terms of *Homo economicus*, we ask ourselves whether populism represents an example of the survival of *Homo politicus* that might even counteract the sacrificial logic of neoliberalism.

We are interested in exploring Brown's notion of sacrifice, since it helps us to think through whether the sacrificial dimension of neoliberalism is not merely a novel reiteration of the sacrificial logic of fascism. As we saw in Essay 2, fascism believes that, in order to govern and guarantee order, it needs to rebuild the lost unity of the community, and that this loss, in turn, was caused by the intrusion of an external presence that threatens it from within. The other – whether immigrant, peasant, indigenous, black, woman, gay, lesbian, or trans – functions as a unity-disturbing element and is therefore culpable for preventing the community from becoming transparent to itself. In this way, fascism plays with the fantasy of being able to achieve the one-people, a people without antagonisms or differences, where the elimination of that threatening figure both exempts the community from guilt and debt while restoring its lost fullness. With this fantasy, the other becomes the sacrificial object allowing for the restoration of the community, and sacrificing the other thus becomes the only action that will guarantee the desired recomposition of the disrupted order.

Now, under neoliberal practices, blame is displaced. Culpability for this impossible fullness is no longer located in the other, but in oneself. We could say that if, under fascism, blame and debt require collective work to identify a sacrificial subject – those who prevent the community from "being fully itself" – under neoliberalism, by contrast, that guilt and debt is privatized. Neoliberal subjectivity and its purported econo-mization of every last corner of life would seem to coincide with the religious gesture of making every individual solely responsible for all the ills that afflict them. Therefore, the illusory search for the recomposition of lost unity no longer comes from the community, but from the individual itself. In other words, the new sacrificial object is no longer the other but oneself, or that part of oneself that, by not allowing us to experience ourselves as complete, must be expelled through very precise practices indicated by the market. And so the subject will be submerged in the obligation – constant, because it is always unsuccessful – to remedy his own lack, to carry out those practices of the self that would allow it to recompose the desired self-identity.

While it is true that populism interpellates every individual as the subject of a lack – the experience of a lack that gives rise to the inscription of a demand – and that in this, as Villacañas warned, it would seem to coincide with neoliberalism, the big difference is that this lack does not function as a mechanism for economistic interpellation. In other words, it does not turn this lack into an ethic of responsibility forcing every individual to position themselves as an entrepreneur of their own life, to try to rid themselves of this constitutive incompleteness. On the contrary, in populist logic, lack does not function as a tool for exploiting the labor power of every individual, but instead becomes a collective political demand – i.e. the constitutive lack or incompleteness that each subject discovers in their singularity becomes the condition of possibility for building a world with others. Thus, popular or political demands do not seek satisfaction on an individual level, but instead serve as a detour that transforms the private practices of every individual – a figure constructed by liberalism and neoliberalism – into practices of the collective political subject that is the people. And this collective possibility reactivates imaginaries associated with the popular will or popular sovereignty – all those imaginaries that neoliberalism wants to make disappear behind the figure of *Homo economicus*.

Regarding the link between the state and subjects, populism helps us reactivate the idea that it is possible to process political demands constructed at the popular level through the state. The state is therefore not reduced to a mere manager of market health, but, instead, by embracing the inherently political dimension of the state's role, populism tries to keep alive democratic imaginaries of social justice, equality, and political freedom. And here we would go beyond Brown, because populist institutions, in addition to keeping *Homo politicus* alive, seem to articulate a novel link between the popular, law, and institutions, a link that takes the form of popular resistance to neoliberalism. All of which seems to lead us to a new problem: namely, the republican dimension of populism – i.e. trying to understand what type of republic this form of political articulation would be able to construct.

Essay 4

Profaning the Public: The Plebeian Dimension of Republican Populism

Is populism anti-institutionalist?

Thinking about the republican dimension of populism means reversing one of the most deeply rooted prejudices in the field of contemporary political thought: the insistence that populism is the antithesis of institutions and the law. Furthermore, this claim is often accompanied by the accusation that populism is responsible for destroying institutions by replacing them with the decisionist figure of a demagogic and manipulative leader.[1] A Manichean opposition is thereby created between the purely decisional (leader) and purely institutional (procedure) dimensions, as if the decisional scope of populism constitutively excludes the institutional dimension of republics.

In this essay, we hope to show how abstract these kinds of statements are, since, if we pay attention to actually existing populisms, we can confirm the coexistence of different types of institutional experiences and decision-making instances. As a result, establishing an external relationship between the decision and the institutions a priori does not help us understand the real link between the two. This implies moving beyond anti-institutionalist readings of populism – and even beyond Laclau himself, since by placing more emphasis on the instituent dimension of populism (the ruptural moment outside institutions), Laclau relegates the instituted dimension (when populism reaches institutions) to the background.[2] What happens if we begin to think that the ruptural (or instituent) logic of populism might be capable of instituting other forms of institutionality? What type of institutions would these be? Could we speak of alternative institutional forms to neoliberalism?

Before exploring these questions, we need to delve more deeply into anti-institutionalist readings of populism in order to show their difficulties. In this regard, the distinction between the ontic and ontological dimensions of populism mentioned in Essays 1 and 2 can now help us to better understand the issue. Most ontic studies of populism are more interested in determining the "populist content" of particular historical experiences in their political conjunctures than in examining the assumptions on which theories of populism are based. The problem is that this approach combines the descriptive and the normative levels in a confused way (Ionescu and Gellner, 1970), attempting to study "concrete" examples of populism in order to determine, on the *level of the given*, a series of characteristics that should be *normatively* applicable to all cases.

The ambivalence of this attitude lies in the fact that, although it is based on the assumption that the given represents a privileged locus for constructing an explanatory model, a series of presuppositions determines how this analysis will be carried out. As a result, a comprehensive evaluative model for dealing with the "populist fact" already invisibly exists. We could say that this way of thinking about populism, although it does not extend to all cases, inherits the prejudices of positivism – namely: making the "facts" a neutral space that invisibilizes the political position of those configuring the very way of describing *the thing*, and thereby constructing those facts themselves. At the end of the day, it seems like the goal is to create a "catalogue" of populist practices to then "apply" to a given reality to see whether it meets the pre-established requirements. Thus, the anti-institutional character of populism preemptively established by most studies functions as a constitutive a priori, waiting to be demonstrated in all cases studied within the empirical field. What is not always problematized here is what kind of role and what characteristics institutions are expected to fulfill such that we could say that populism is incapable of incorporating them. The insistence that populism is anti-institutional by nature therefore conceals an absolute vagueness about how we understand institutions and what would make them legitimate or illegitimate. In other words, the locus of enunciation that preemptively determines how we should understand institutions is invisibilized.

From an ontological point of view, there also seems to be some difficulty in thinking about the institutional dimension of populism. The first thing to be rescued here is the need to think more about how populist logic is articulated than about its empirical content. This doesn't mean neglecting the ontic dimension, but it does mean being aware of its dependence on the ontological. Now, while Laclau was one of the first thinkers to raise this difference, he has not given us enough tools to think ontologically about the institutional aspect of populism, which often leaves us trapped in the liberal perspective of procedural democracy or in political apathy, according to which institutions are a procedural mechanism in the hands of experts, far from the conflict, leadership, passions, and affections of political life. That is why it is important to explore what happens to the logic of political articulation in the experience of populist governmentality, especially when it is traversed by affects and leadership. The first question we can ask is: does the role of affects and leadership necessarily entail an absence of rationality or citizenship and a contempt for institutions? Or is it the lens we are looking through that makes us believe this? And even if we go further and think about why so many reject this insistence on the role of affects and leaders, we find that these two dimensions reveal not only the conflictive nature of politics, but also the fact that the political nature of institutions is associated with an incalculable excess.

It therefore seems necessary for us to to highlight the political position that gives rise to and sustains these false dichotomies, and which reacts against the conflictive dimension of the social. Mouffe is one of the contemporary thinkers who has sought most lucidly to untangle this knot of prejudice. Her early reflections on ideology (Mouffe, 1991: 167–227) and later writings on democracy (1993) clearly indicate the role of affects in the construction of hegemonic identifications and projects in democracies. Following Mouffe, we can easily detect an entire consensual matrix (which we will call liberal) behind the rejection or pejorative understanding of populism, which runs the risk of embracing post-political discourse when thinking about institutions.

On the other hand, since populist theory is an exercise that renders visible the *decision* inherent in political praxis, it highlights the narrow-mindedness of political scientists who reduce democratic institutions to two variables: the vote of citizens and the procedure of experts. This simplified view of institutions as a rule to be followed according to a series of previously regulated procedures means that any decision-making dimension is considered an affront to democracy. It therefore seems important to warn that populist practices, far from rejecting institutions and the democratic game, take them up in a more complex way – namely, by drawing attention to the decisional and affective dimension of political praxis (whether within or outside the institutions), thereby undermining the lofty vision of those who prioritize the consensual and procedural dimension of democracy.

If populist theory allows us to understand one thing it is that the moment of decision is *ineradicable*, something that post-political discourse, through a restricted view of institutions, reason, and pluralism, seeks to conceal.[3] What is troubling is: why would making this decisional and conflictive element clear entail institutional weakness? Would the automation of institutional procedure be healthier? And isn't procedure an invisibilized form of decision anyway? Hasn't the crisis of European social democracy been the best proof of the fallacy on which the belief in a procedural democracy allegedly indifferent to decisionism was based?

Doesn't this crisis reflect the entire chain of arbitrariness decided in the name of procedural democracies?

Ruptural institutionality

Once we have interrogated the arguments for populism being anti-institutionalist, we can assert that a non-liberal view of institutions can help us conceptualize populist institutionality, by abandoning the straitjacket through which contemporary forms of institutionality tend to be theorized. But it also forces us to understand two things: on the one hand, that ontic studies offering some tools for thinking through the relationship between institutions and populism – associated, above all, with sociology – lose sight of the fact that the process of institutionalization must be understood through the link between the demands of social organizations and the state. Neglecting this link between social demands and the state undermines what findings can be made vis-à-vis populist institutionality, while leaning toward a negative reading of the purportedly authoritarian or anti-democratic role populism grants to institutions (Germani, 2019; Zanatta, 2005). And, on the other hand, we need to understand that those ontological theorizations linking the democratizing role of populism to its antagonistic and ruptural dimension tend to emphasize the organizational capacity of social mobilization rooted exclusively outside institutions.

To escape this impasse, we need to reconsider the almost mechanical identification of institutions with "those on top" (differential logic) and populism with "those on the bottom" (logic of equivalence) (Laclau, 2005a: 80–2). Let's not forget that Laclau identifies differential logic with the status quo and the satisfaction of demands through institutional procedures, encouraging the idea that the institutional sphere is not connected to the logical equivalence of populist articulation. If we consider the problems posed on both the ontic and ontological levels, we can say that we are facing a theoretical dilemma. On the one hand, we have sociological studies dedicated to thinking through populist institutional experiences in terms of anti-democratic authoritarianism, and on the other hand, we have democratizing theorizations of populism from an anti-institutional perspective. The challenge is to theorize a democratic populist institutionality.

Toward this end, we consider the possibility of a populist institutionality built by "those on the bottom" in terms of a *type of institutional articulation* that has been little explored up to this point – namely, *as the institution of rights* (and their respective popular uses). This is the kind of articulation that has characterized the governments of Cristina Fernández de Kirchner (2007–15), Rafael Correa (2008–17), Evo Morales (2006–19), and Lula da Silva (2003–10). It is a type of articulation that allows us to theorize a linkage between popular demands and institutions that, even though it might have a decisional aspect, escapes the logic of anti-institutional immediacy. This instance makes intelligible a form of articulation between political leaders and popular demands that takes as its object of inquiry the egalitarian aspect of institutions (Coronel and Cadahia, 2018). According to this framework, institutions (the state) should not be understood as a mechanism that segments and orders demands for their individual satisfaction, but rather as one that incorporates the contentious dimension of equivalential logic to compete with those on top for these same (oligarchic or popular) state forms. In other words, the state (and institutions) become another antagonistic space in the dispute between those on the bottom and those on top. At the same time, this forces us to reconsider a series of issues having to do with social mobilization, institutions, and the link between the two.

It is very common to understand social mobilization through its capacity to come together around a "dissatisfaction" and to configure it as a popular demand. Research on social movements has emphasized how a social link is positivized (the demand) out of a negativity (the failure of the state). But if it is a populist government that takes up the demand (or even helps to build it) and introduces it antagonistically into the institutions until it becomes a right, would we be simply talking about a differential logic in Laclauian terms? Or would it be another specific kind of differential logic that has not yet been elaborated with the rigor the case demands? Doesn't the practical logic of populism bring to the fore the decisional, antagonistic, and contentious dimension inherent in all institutional practices? For all these reasons, it might be time to abandon the liberal perspective – which assumes that institutions are the antithesis of decisionism and conflict – and delve more deeply into that other tradition that has thought about institutions differently. We refer to the old legacy of republicanism.

Plebeian republicanism

Although the tradition of republican thought can refer back to the Greeks (Bertomeu, 2015), we are interested in setting out from contemporary debates, and specifically those related to the link between conflict, institutions, and freedom. Without wanting to simplify the discussion, we could say that there exists a tension within studies on republicanism that rests on a bifurcation between a liberal and a popular republicanism (Domènech, 2004). The first seeks to combine the premises of classical liberalism – methodological individualism, the division of powers, and negative freedom – with a reflection on republican institutions and how they might serve to guarantee these principles. This type of link tries to focus on the consensual dimension of institutions and abandons a feature that will be key for the other route: conflict and the forms of organization associated with popular sovereignty. From this perspective, conflict is therefore experienced as a flaw or weakness of institutions and democracy, and its existence as a sign of their deterioration. Hence one of the best representatives of this view, Philip Petit (1999), has promoted deliberative republicanism in order to be able to dialogically discern between arbitrary and non-arbitrary interventions by institutions – i.e. to be able to determine consensually when a state should intervene to guarantee the republican freedom of its citizens, and when it should not. Populism, as an experience that builds power through conflict, would be seen by this liberal republican current as the antithesis of any institutional project. But if we focus on those investigations that identify republicanism with popular power, it is possible to establish a fruitful encounter with populism.

We distance ourselves from liberal republicanism since it tends to understand republicanism as a means to dissolve antagonism, assuming that the freedom of citizens is accomplished through consensus and conflict resolution. Against this view, we are interested in rescuing, on the one hand, the interpretations of the "Atlantic republican tradition" popularized by the Cambridge School's reading of Machiavelli's (2003) Florentine republicanism, and, on the other, the "continental republicanism" distinguished by Althusser and Negri through the republicanism of Spinoza and Marx (Negri, 1999, 2000, 2008, 2013; Althusser, 2006, 2011). This is because the Atlantic and continental traditions share the assumption that it is not so much a question of eradicating conflict as one of the possibility of managing it through institutions and democracy (Rinesi and Muraca, 2010: 63–6). The first current allows us to see that, since Machiavelli – who maintained that there exist in every society "two diverse humors, that of the people and that of the great" (Machiavelli, 1996: 16) – conflict has functioned as a means to achieve the freedom of citizens (Skinner, 1978, 1981), and even to help improve the laws and institutions that guarantee that freedom and allow its expansion (cf. Rinesi and Muraca, 2010: 65). The second current, for its part, helps us to think about how social antagonisms allow for a transformation of society toward an equality that would promote true freedom.

Now, in both Latin America and Spain, academics like Julia Bertomeu (2015), Eduardo Rinesi (2015, 2018; Rinesi and Muraca, 2010), Ailynn Torres Santana (2018), Julio Guanche (2018), Valeria Coronel and Luciana Cadahia (2018), Daniel Raventós (2005), and Antoni Domènech (2004), have inherited these Atlantic and continental approaches and are revitalizing research on republicanism through an underexplored aspect: its plebeian dimension. Within these new studies, we can distinguish between, on the one hand, research aimed at establishing a link between socialism and republicanism, and, on the other, those studies seeking to connect republicanism to populism, without ignoring the pioneering nature of socialist research. But, above all, there is a clear need to distinguish between two kinds of republic: an oligarchic and aristocratic republic versus a democratic and plebeian one (Bertomeu, 2015; Rinesi, 2018). As the scholar of republicanism Julia Bertomeu suggests: "Republicanism is an ancient tradition, deeply rooted in the classical ancient Mediterranean, and commonly and rightly associated with the names Ephialtes, Pericles, Protagoras, and Democritus (in its democratic-plebeian form) and those of Aristotle and Cicero (in its anti-democratic form)" (2015). In the modern world, Bertomeu adds, it also reappears in these same two variants: a democratic one (which seeks the universalization of republican freedom and the consequent inclusion of the poor majority as citizens) and an anti-democratic one (which seeks to exclude from civic and political life those who live by their hands, granting a monopoly on political power to wealthy property-owners).

If we follow the thread of Bertomeu's argument, it is difficult to speak of republicanism "plain and simple," and not just any form of republicanism would be desirable in and of itself. Through these two counterposed genealogies of republicanism, both Bertomeu and Antoni Domènech – another scholar of the link between republicanism and socialism – point out that what distinguishes the two is the role assigned to property and law. Anti-democratic republicanism, these authors tell us, seeks to configure a republic that consists of a small number of property-owners, in which the law would play a dual role: as a mechanism to preserve the privileges of a minority, while at the same time dispossessing the majority. In this way, the alleged universalizability of republican freedom would be deceptive, since only those whose material conditions of existence are guaranteed would be able to enjoy it. Those without access to property, by contrast, are relegated to formal freedom not guaranteed by the republic.

Furthermore, from this perspective, institutions function as a mechanism to perpetuate dispossession and inequality

(Bertomeu, 2005; Domènech, 2004; Raventós, 2005). When we think of the systematic deaths of social movement leaders fighting to preserve their territories in places like Colombia, Brazil, Mexico, and Central America,[4] we can observe more clearly the operation of this kind of anti-democratic republicanism. These leaders fight for the use of their lands (properties) and are assassinated through para-state alliances[5] to strip them of these lands and, in some cases, turn them over to transnational corporations. This clear exercise of land dispossession also entails a dispossession of citizenship by the state, guaranteeing the privilege of property to a small few and depriving the majority of their right and freedom to make use of the land. On the other hand, these authors help us think about the link with property that this type of republicanism promotes. In his 2004 book *The Eclipse of Fraternity*, Antoni Domènech tells us that, although modernity involved the destruction of feudalism's patriarchal and paternalistic way of life, it nevertheless maintained the property bond of the feudal lord within the domestic sphere – namely, a bond of absolute authority. This meant that, while in the public sphere each property-owner would be a free citizen of the republic, in the private sphere, by contrast, he would be master of all that he took as his own: his lands, workers, wife, and children. Or, in other words, patriarchy was eliminated in equal treatment vis-à-vis other citizens as property-owners, but preserved in domestic relations toward the dispossessed (worker, woman, indigenous, black, etc.).

Democratic or popular republicanism, on the other hand, would indeed seek to universalize republican freedom, since, as Bertomeu and Domènech help us to see, this form of republicanism cannot be understood without the problem of equality. In other words, if we are all equal, there is no way to justify inequality within a republic, and, similarly, the law and institutions cannot be understood as the property and privilege of the few, but as mechanisms for expanding the rights of the majority. It is thus assumed that, in a republic, we are all citizens, and therefore that mechanisms of inequality and dispossession should be fought by the state and the law. Along these lines, we could wonder whether or not populist experiences in Latin America have been a way of extending the law, institutions, and freedom to historically excluded sectors that for a long time have been demanding the *right to have rights* (Rinesi, 2015).

Toward a republican populism?

For some time now, distinct efforts have been made to put the debates on populism and republicanism within the same constellation. One of the first authors to establish this reconciliation was Carlos Vilas, who in 2009 ventured to describe populism as "a kind of practical republicanism insofar as it raises the flag of the primacy of the interests and the well-being of the whole (people, nation, homeland) over and above private interests and privileges, and is expressed in the institutionalization of a wide range of social and economic rights and public regulations" (2009).[6] But it is Eduardo Rinesi who has made a stronger claim by declaring that Latin American populism is the form through which republicanism has developed in Latin America (Rinesi and Muraca, 2010: 59–76).

When wondering about the antagonistic nature of populism, Rinesi tells us, alongside Muraca, that this is because "the word people [*pueblo*] defines a *particular* collective subject, the identity *of the poor*, and its 'consensualist,' organicist, and harmonizing component (which is often reproached by critics on the 'left')," but that it is also associated "with the fact that the same word 'people' *also* defines a *universal* collective subject, the identity of all members of the social body as a whole" (Rinesi and Muraca, 2010: 64). The people thereby reveals an excess, its irresolvable tension as both a "part" and "the whole." However, Rinesi tells us, it would be deceptive to believe that this tension is located within the people, since it is through this word that we arrive at the heart of politics itself, given that "there is politics precisely *because* this tension exists (that *tension* and that *pretension*: the [pre]tension of a part that wants to be the whole and the simultaneous affirmation of a whole – which moreover has the same name as that pretentious part – that denies that part, and any part, the right to such a pretension)" (65).

Rinesi, citing Lefort, discovers this form of conflict – this irreducible antagonism that produces a fundamental division within the social – in the classic republicanism of authors like Machiavelli (Rinesi and Muraca, 2010: 65). Furthermore, Rinesi warns, republican freedom and institutions originate – and gain their permanence – thanks to disunity, conflict, and social division:

> Thus the republic exists because, thanks to institutions and laws, there exists a field, a terrain, a common horizon, a space that, so to speak, belongs to everyone, that is *universal*. But at the same time a republic only exists ... when this common field is a field ... of *battle*: a field where we encounter (in the double sense of coming together and *confronting*) the *conflicting* desires, interests, and values of different social sectors, of the different *particularities* that, in an irremediably conflictive way, constitute the social body. (Rinesi and Muraca, 2010: 66)

It is on the basis of this reading that Rinesi opens up the question of whether "it would not be a worthwhile theoretical exercise to try to think these two theoretical and political traditions – republicanism and populism – *together*, to articulate their categories (which are not so different) and their logics (which are the same)" (Rinesi and Muraca, 2010: 73). If we pay attention to the game that he proposes to us, we can understand that this conflictual reading leads him to a bold interpretation: namely, to consider republican questions like "the common good," "public happiness," and "justice" to be chimeras – in light of the inherently conflictual nature of the "thing," the *res publica* – and to what extent this litigious dimension is precisely what keeps institutions and freedom *alive* (Rinesi and Muraca, 2010: 73).

On the basis of Rinesi's proposal to think of populism and republicanism jointly, it seems interesting to begin speaking in terms of a *republican populism* as the antithesis of neoliberalism, as a way of naming one of the ways that plebeian republicanism has been taking shape in Latin America. This entails understanding the republican dimension of populism within the broader temporal arc of the democratic revolutions in Latin America and the Caribbean, since this gesture of uniting citizenship and plebeian struggles represents a part of the contentious history of our continent (James, 2001; Sanders, 2004; Lasso, 2007).

Therefore, populism should be theorized from Global South academic institutions in accordance with historiographic and political science research that seeks to draw attention to a history of popular institutionality that runs parallel to the official story of the oligarchic and exclusionary nation-states inherited from colonial rule. As if Latin American and Caribbean independence secretly inaugurated two forms of institutionality and citizenship, two ways of thinking about the role of the state and the law, two competing historical forces split between the construction of an unequal and elitist society and an egalitarian popular society. Understood this way, then, contemporary populism could be thought of as the attempt to reactivate that old democratic revolutionary legacy today, through the constituent assemblies of the Andes and the populisms of the Southern Cone.

We are referring to that old legacy set into motion beginning with the Haitian Revolution and the profoundly transgressive gesture of saying, on a continent dominated by slavery and colonialism, that: "All citizens, from now on, shall be known by the generic denomination of blacks" (Article 14 of the Haitian Constitution of 1805). That is to say, when black slaves became conscious of the fact that they too had the right to have rights, and, even more so, when they assumed that, that it was their responsibility to universalize the secret of plebeian republics: that there can be no truly republican freedom if it is not possible to build equality. So, faced with the conception of property that perpetuates links of inequality within oligarchic and anti-democratic republicanism, our legacies of plebeian republicanism instead seek to destroy and desecrate the last remnant of patriarchal property: the belief that the property relation legitimizes some type of *dominion* – and thereby dispossession – over nature, oneself, and others. If nobody can claim the right to possess and dispossess others as they please, it is because the *res publica*, far from being the exclusive dominion of some, is instead a social bond that we build among everyone, through an egalitarian commitment.

Essay 5
Toward an Internationalist Populism

The beautiful souls of pure causes

It is very common to find in academic spaces an almost immediate aversion to the link that populism builds between the figure of the people and that of the leader. One of the most common arguments, stemming from both the liberal and autonomist socialist traditions, consists of warning us about the identitarian nationalisms that are forged around this relationship. While we showed in Essays 2 and 3 that the logic of political articulation that populism proposes does not give shape to the identitarian danger that many warn about, we still need to develop more precisely the question of nationalism that seems to nest within the link between the people and the leader – more than anything because this feature of populism could function as its own limit, as a kind of border preventing it from building an internationalist alternative beyond the narrow and closed circle of the state. So it seems important, first of all, for us to try to understand better how this relationship is configured and how unfounded many of the prejudices associated with it are, and, second, to show what kind of a nation populism allows us to think and why it is able to maintain – against what the detractors say – an internationalist openness.

The first thing to note is that the figure of the leader should not be limited to a head of state, as critics of populism often see it, but should instead be taken up in a broader sense to include those we have called social movement or territorial leaders in Latin America and the Caribbean. Figures like Berta Cáceres in Honduras, Francia Márquez in Colombia, Marielle Franco in Brazil, Evo Morales in Bolivia, Rafael Correa in Ecuador, Gustavo Petro in Colombia, and Cristina Fernández de Kirchner in Argentina – to name a few contemporary examples – are part of a long tradition of building popular leadership in Latin America and the Caribbean.[1] This broadening of the meaning of the word "leader" allows us to move away from the old Eurocentric imaginary fixated on hackneyed figures like Napoleon, Hitler, and Mussolini, while helping us to think about the question of Latin American leadership according to its own logic and without preconceptions forged in other latitudes.

It is not insignificant to recall the historical disdain that even authors like Marx displayed for the complex figure of Simón Bolívar. Nor should we forget that, once the experiences of European totalitarianism had ended, a belief was projected – as if through a sort of upside-down mirror – that dictators of all political stripes are actually manufactured in peripheral countries and not in old Europe. Isn't the famous genre of the Latin American dictator novel[2] one of the most consolidated forms of European colonialism, and of the blindness of certain political positions that prevents popular power built on the basis of plebeian leadership from being legible? We could ask ourselves whether the animosity toward Latin American and Caribbean leaders does not rest on some archetypes specific to the European colonial mentality, which finds it incredibly difficult to grant any sort of rationality and political possibility to these types of figures that have always oscillated between social mobilization and political parties. Furthermore, some of the figures who have become heads of state, like Evo Morales, built their leadership thanks to their participation in a social or territorial movement.[3]

By broadening the idea of the leader, the historical persecution of political and social leaders in Latin America thereby becomes clearer, a phenomenon spanning from the systematic planning of murders – as occurs in Central America, Colombia, and Brazil – to judicial persecution, juridical coups, and imprisonment – as has been occurring in Ecuador, Argentina, and Brazil. Oligarchies can no longer resort to the civilian–military coups of the 1950s, 1960s, and 1970s, but are now capable of generating the same effects from within the juridical logic of the rule of law. Or, put another way, the Latin American right can now systematically murder and persecute leaders without interrupting the democratic narrative.

Therefore, the first question we would like to ask those in the academy who feel such hostility toward these leaders is the following: what do they think motivates this persecution, and don't they find it to be a major coincidence that, when a political, social, or territorial leader becomes critical of neoliberalism, persecution, smears, and, in the worst cases, imprisonment or death almost automatically come into play? Now it is we who wonder what kind of secret power these leaders must personify in their flesh that makes them so unbearable for the current world order? And we also broaden this concern by daring to ask what role the academy plays when professors – from their comfortable offices, and distant from political praxis – disdainfully observe or reject the actions of a leader, reproducing in their assessment all the stereotypes historically associated with Eurocentric epistemic colonialism.

Let's dig a little deeper into this prejudice to understand more thoroughly what kind of threat the figure of the leader must pose to the health of a republic. Here we find a return to the old metaphysical opposition between the idea and the body. The idea, or the regulatory ideal – if we put it in modern terms – functions as a sort of uncontaminated ideal archetype that finds contemporary expression in categories like "correct institutional procedure," "technocratic values," "the rule of law," and "the common will." In all these cases, the same symptom operates: namely, the belief that there is a kind of order beyond the decisional instance – i.e. an order that depends not on the singular corporality of the one making a decision, but on an abstract force operating outside of any singularity. This is how we can understand abstract ideas like neutral institutions (liberalism), effective market procedure (technocracy), and the harmonious sum of all singular wills (autonomist socialism). The problem with these beliefs is that they seem to share the same ontology: the existence of a non-contingent order, an order that exists outside of our here-and-now, so that any singular incarnation – any corporality that takes up that order – does nothing but contaminate it, betray it, and stain the purity of its origin.

Now, this diffuse defense of autonomy (or of some abstract idea of the common or social good) seems to take for granted the existence of a superiority of ideals that are themselves beyond or above the flesh of any person who leads. Any political formation – which prides itself on being effectively rational and rigorously consistent – instead of having a preponderant leader, should instead uphold an idea in that place, e.g. the concept of social democracy, socialism, or communism, etc. Thus, a proper and serious political formation would be defined by being bound together by a concept – likely institutionalized in a political party or some kind of political or social organization – with members following this or that idea, independent of leadership.

The presence of a leader, the mere possibility that a political project might be embodied in a corporality traversed by time and its finitude, seems to set off all the alarm bells. On the one hand, this is because, when a leader linked to a people emerges hoisting the banner of an emancipatory political project, for many it immediately evokes the specter of terror. These alarm bells are rung in proportion to the fear that every collective project perched upon this link will always contain in its most intimate folds the possibility of unleashing authoritarianism, or, in the worst of cases, totalitarian horror. If the relationship of political projects among peoples remains under the influence of a leader, then everything would be in the hands of the moods or sympathies of the moment, setting aside the durability and stability afforded by building upon abstract principles.

The real trap – the unconfessed secret behind these views that make the leader into an extremely dangerous figure – is the belief that there is something to preserve and an order to follow. Believing that this exists, therefore, they fear that an individual might want to appropriate this secret and convince the people that this abstract idea or regulatory ideal can live in their own finite body. However, according to the theory of populism that we are trying to develop here, there is no such thing as an ideal to "preserve" against the betrayal by a leader, but rather this leader is the failed personification of the irreplaceable, of what could be but is not yet. The leader is the figure who, through their corporality, positivizes popular articulations that are rooted in the radically contingent, negative, and indeterminate nature of social being.

Despite the antipathy that the figure of the leader generates, in this regard we follow Mouffe's position that "it is very difficult to find examples of important political movements without prominent leaders" (2018: 70). What's more, we could add that even those experiences, historical or theoretical, that sought to capture concretely, or think through, mechanisms for achieving the greatest possible horizontality had to appeal to a leader at some point. And this is as old as the very idea of the West, whose Athenian democracy in its golden age had a leader of the stature of Pericles (c.495–429 BC). So we are going to leave aside for a moment the prejudices around the relationship between people and leader, and work more carefully through the secret of this link as seen through the lenses of populist theory.

The people and its leader

When thinking about the people, it becomes essential to pause over two conceptual distinctions that detractors of populism often confuse. In the first place, it is fundamental not to conflate the people of populism with the Freudian mass or group. Second, it is important not to conflate the Freudian group with the primal horde, because this confusion is what has led many to analogize the populist leader to the father of the primal horde, to understand the leader – erroneously – through the Freudian metaphor of *Totem and Taboo* (1990a [1913–14]).[4]

Let's begin with the conceptual distinction between the Freudian group and the people. When Laclau (2005a) revisited the key texts on mass psychology, he found that these were based on two assumptions, from which the phenomenon of the masses was then constructed as an aberration. We refer in the first place to the assumption that the normal/pathological binary pair corresponds to the opposition between rational forms of social organization and mass phenomena, associating the former with the normal and the latter with the pathological. And, second, that the rationality/irrationality pair corresponds to the contrast between the individual and the group, binding irrationality to group formations. These highly popular binary oppositions – for example, in works by Gustave Le Bon (1896) and Hippolyte Taine (1878) – were not destabilized until Freud's theoretical intervention, which, according to Laclau, produced "the most radical breakthrough which had so far been accomplished in mass psychology" (2005a: 52).

Freud, in a deconstructive gesture already present at the beginning of his book *Group Psychology and the Analysis of the Ego* (1990 [1920–2]), rejected the sharp separation between individual psychology and social psychology, since the other is always a constitutive element of the psychic apparatus. So he proposed that the individual/group tandem should not be treated as an exclusive relationship between opposite poles, but as a complex relationship, insofar as the social always cuts across the constitution of subjectivity.[5] Laclau followed this gesture in order to relativize accusations that populism is irrational or pathological, and accompanied the traces left by Freud to develop his notion of the people, but he did so without thereby connecting it to the notion of the group. Laclau – like Freud – set aside the idea of suggestion or manipulation to explain group unity, and placed affect and the libidinal bond in a decisive position for grasping the nature of the social bond. In any case, "the social bond would be a libidinal bond; as such, it relates to everything that concerns 'love'" (Laclau, 2005a: 53).

Let's keep in mind that, in order to study groups, and thus to be able to establish how the libidinal bond operates in collective phenomena, Freud took as paradigmatic the type of group that is highly organized, durable, artificial, and has a *leader*. He drew two conclusions from his work on the cases of the church and the army: first, that each individual has a double libidinal bond, with the leader on the one hand, and with other members of the group on the other. Second, that what is essential about the group and what provides its unity is affect. And that, in this double bond, the libidinal tie to the leader is essential, so much so that the bond falls apart in the absence of that tie. This is the case because, in characterizing the two directions of the libidinal bond, Freud showed that the bond between members of the group should be understood in terms of identification. Among the different types of identification, Freud refers to the promotion of a link born of sharing a quality with a person who is not the object of sexual drives, and in the case of the group this shared quality is love for the leader.[6] In turn, Freud indicates that the link between each group member and the leader should be understood in terms of idealization or being in love (the lover transfers a considerable part of the narcissistic libido to the loved object; by locating the object in the place of the ideal, the lover affectively invests in the object as he did with his own ego in the narcissistic phase).

Now, this is where Laclau takes a detour that allows him to establish a distinction between the mass or group and the people, through a two-step argument: first following Freud, and then distancing himself. First, Laclau finds another form of social aggregation in Freud's own text that is distinct from that involved in the case of the group with a leader – i.e. the double directionality of the libidinal bond. This is the form of grouping that "by means of too much 'organization'" can "acquire secondarily the characteristics of an individual" (1990 [1920–2]: 80).[7] Second, distancing himself from Freud, Laclau asserted that these two ways of establishing a group (the group with a leader, and an organization) do not correspond to two different types of groups (as Freud argued) but to two logics of aggregation present in the constitution of all social groups. This conclusion was crucial for grasping populism, because then Laclau could insist that the people should never be understood as a social aggregation that is bound together solely by a libidinal investment (identification and idealization), but that it also entails organization.

From there, a first distinction between group and people arises. The populist people is not a political articulation composed of merely libidinal ties, but is also made up of organizations. We insist that the people is not only made up of love for the leader and identification among its members: it is also composed of a variety of organizations. The people includes unions, political parties, and the most diverse forms of social movements (social clubs, neighborhood associations, human rights organizations, student centers, groups chaired by village priests, LGBT+ and feminist groupings, etc.). Therefore, the people cannot be understood as an undifferentiated mass of individuals held together purely by the libidinal tie. The people is never the same as soccer fans, an angry mob, or a sum of individuals who have fallen under the hypnotic influence of a captivating leader.

Strangely, there is an image that is usually pointed to as irrefutable proof by those who defend the identity between the Freudian group and the people, which from our perspective seems to prove entirely the opposite. We refer to photos of the populist plazas of Kirchnerism that on numerous occasions brought the leader and her people together at the geographic heart of Argentina's great political rallies – the Plaza de Mayo in Buenos Aires – between 2007 and 2015. If we pay close attention, we see how President Cristina Fernández de Kirchner walks into a plaza that is full of people, but also overflowing with innumerable different insignia referring to the variety of organizations present, and with banners testifying to membership in, or sympathy for, different organizations. This practice of public expression, which is absolutely widespread in Argentina, shows that, far from an undifferentiated mass under the influence of a leader who manipulates it at will, we instead witness in these political rallies the constitution of a people that manifests and articulates itself in pursuit of a series of demands through a variety of organizations.

We can also refer to another, less well-known image: the presence of the Colombian people at the scene of Jorge Eliecer Gaitán's murder. The assassination, the confirmation by the people of their leader's absence, and their powerlessness to convert their demands into state policy all laid the foundations for extending the struggle through popular organizing outside the institutions. This gave rise to one of Colombia's most controversial moments: the April 9, 1948 *Bogotazo*, and the subsequent conformation of the liberal guerrillas of Marquetalia (today the Revolutionary Armed Forces of Colombia – FARC).

A second fundamental distinction between the group and the people is that, while in the Freudian schema the group articulates psychic instances, in Laclau's schema the people articulates demands. And we must not forget that the inscription of a demand presupposes a complexity in which the desire of the subjects is implicated. Following Lacan, Laclau takes the demand to be an operation in two parts that are bound together: need and desire.[8] The people is thus a political subjectivity constituted through the articulation of different equivalent demands that are bound together in an empty signifier, or a demand capable of containing the others (the name of the leader).

With these two distinctions in mind, we can say that the people implies the construction of a complex web connecting the equivalence of demands in relation to a leader and the absorption of those same demands through organization, i.e. institutionalized forms of absorption. It is thus worth returning at this point to the widespread idea that populism can only exist as such in a position of opposition, as an expression of anti-status-quo sentiment that only promotes the destabilization of the established order, the disruption of institutionalized forms of exchange. Perhaps what underlies this type of interpretation of populism is an ignorance of the organizational dimension of constituting the people. In this regard, we have already argued the opposite in Essay 4: that populism goes beyond the mere moment of rupture – it also generates institutions and creates the republic. So it is not simply about understanding populism only in its antagonistic aspect, because, from the outset, the people is also made up of a fabric of institutions.

But there is still a third aspect that we should mention when distinguishing the group from the people. Let's return for a moment to the theorization of the libidinal tie central to constituting the Freudian group. Following Biglieri and Perelló (2012), we can see how Laclau rescues from Freud's work the argument that he developed in the sections of *Group Psychology* entitled "A Differentiating Grade in the Ego" and "Postscript." There, Laclau finds Freud arguing the thesis that the libidinal bond between group members and the leader is not only one of being in love or idealization, but also one of *identification*. In other words, the link with the leader is also endowed with the same type of libidinal bond that operates between *peers*, i.e. other group members. This aspect is key, because what we can immediately deduce is that the leader is always *in pari materia* vis-à-vis the led, a *primus inter pares*. Indeed, if in addition to being in love, the led maintain a bond of identification with the leader, what Freud is proposing – and with which Laclau absolutely agrees – is that the leader and followers share some element (other than sexual drives) that puts them in a position of parity and enables a *mutual bond*.

Hence, if the libidinal bond between the followers and the leader has a double dimension (being in love and identification), the prospect of a purely narcissistic leader is ruled out. Laclau puts it as follows: "as he participates in that very substance of the community which makes identification possible, his identity is split: he is the father, but also one of the brothers" (2005a: 59). And with this he reinforces the idea that the populist leader can never be the narcissistic despotic father who is of the classic imaginary, because, as his link with his followers is forged both by being in love and by identification, his right to lead is based on a shared trait or element that group members recognize as outstanding in him. Thus, the leader is always responsible to and held accountable by the community:

> since his right to rule is based on the recognition by other group members of a feature of the leader which he shares, in a particularly pronounced way, with all of them, the leader is, to a considerable extent, accountable to the community. The need for leadership could still be there – for structural reasons that Freud does not really explore, but to which we shall return in a moment – but it is a far more democratic leadership than the one involved in the notion of the narcissistic despot. We are, in fact, not far away from that peculiar combination of consensus and coercion that Gramsci called hegemony. (Laclau, 2005a: 60)

This leaves us at the gates of our second clarification: the leader of the people is not analogous to the narcissistic father of the primal horde. Often, the populist leader is equated with the father of the horde that Freud uses as a metaphor in *Totem and Taboo* (1990a [1913–14]). Those making this comparison think of an absolute leader who captures for himself all the *enjoyment* that others ultimately *lack*. But those making this analogy lose sight of the fact that the father of the horde corresponds to a logical moment prior to social constitution, so it is clear that he cannot be the same as whoever occupies the place of the leader within an established social formation. In any case, in *Totem and Taboo*, Freud depicts the origin of culture; the authoritarian father of the primal horde had to be killed and devoured by the brothers in order to give rise to the constitution of society and to reconfigure leadership as precisely *a place* and therefore able to be occupied by one of the brothers. Therefore, once the leader's place has been established as such, whoever hopes to occupy that place will always be one of the brothers, a *primus inter pares* who will always be *in the place of the father* but who *will never be the father*. Furthermore, whoever occupies that place will always do so under the threat of being killed by the others.

Having established these two conceptual clarifications that distinguish the people from both the group or mass and the primal horde, it is undeniable that the leader occupies a fundamental place in any populist articulation. The first question that helps us to address this importance can be found if we follow the outline left by Laclau when he states that we cannot understand the place of the leader merely as an empty and neutral space. There is something else there to explore, of course, if we do not want our analysis to be trapped in the formalism implied by the institutionalization of the leader's place (say, for example, the legal dimension and the procedural aspects of democracy, which are, of course, also extremely important). If we also hope to take into account the notion of *politeia* in its full breadth as "a community's whole political way of life, where constitutional arrangements represent only a formal crystallization" (Laclau, 2005a: 169) – to which we could add Mouffe's (1993) argument that this notion also entails the formation of political subjectivities – we must bear in mind that the place of the leader is never unaffected by the antagonisms that historically shaped it, by the elements articulated there by the people, and by who occupies it now and the traces carved by those who occupied it previously. There is a mutual contamination between the person occupying the place of the leader and the very nature of that place.

This contamination is due, on the one hand, to the fact that each new antagonistic setting means inscribing new marks that make that place of the leader always – at some point – a different place. In other words, the place of the leader bears the mark of the populist *plebs* (the hegemonic force) that arrogates for itself the representation of the *populus*. And, on the other hand, it will bear the mark of the person who, through their very body, sets the political articulations of a given context into motion. Someone needs to embody the will of the people, the assembly of the people, the idea, the concept, or the goal. The second issue that tells us about the importance of the leader in populism is associated with the name of the leader and the performative aspect of naming. Laclau refers to the singularity that the name of the leader imprints on the people: "an assemblage of heterogeneous elements kept equivalentially together only by a name is, however, necessarily a *singularity*" (2005a: 100). He also tells us that the name of the leader becomes the foundation of equivalence, since "[i]n this way, almost imperceptibly, the equivalential logic leads to singularity, and singularity to identification of the unity of the group with the name of the leader" (2005a: 100). Therefore, beyond the centrality that leadership acquires for populism, this is never about a merely individual will that disposes of things as it pleases, gaining more or less autocratic features depending on the case. Rather, it is that the name of the populist leader expresses the singularity of a people embodied in the singularity of a body. Once this name becomes the name of the people itself, we can say that we are witnessing the expression of a political subjectivity, a corporality, and a discursive context capable of accounting for the crystallization of a unique political moment traversed by specific antagonisms and demands that are inscribed in historical legacies and shared traditions.

By naming the people, the leader names a collective construct that goes far beyond their own person and opens up to the possibility of a future that does not yet exist. The people far exceeds the leader, to the extent that the latter will never be able to dominate or manipulate at will what that people generates. The proper name goes far beyond the person embodying leadership, to the point that the one does not coincide with the other. Here it is worth bringing up as an example the words delivered by Hugo Chávez Frías in several of his speeches, since they reflect the wisdom of the populist leader regarding his place:

> Chávez you are no longer Chávez. You are a people. Chávez became a people. As the great Colombian leader Gaitán once said, I am no longer truly me, I am no longer me, I am a people and you – this is how I feel – I feel embodied in you. As I said and I will say again: you, Venezuelan girl, are also Chávez. You, Venezuelan boy, are also Chávez. You are also Chávez, worker, grandmother, grandfather. You are also Chávez, Venezuelan child, you too are Chávez. Chávez truly became a people. (Hugo Chávez Frías, Barcelona, Anzoátegui, Venezuela, campaign speech)[9]

Chávez (the person/character) and Chavismo do not coincide with one another. Furthermore, it is not that the people is incarnated in the leader's individuality (narcissistic love), but rather that the people uses the name of the leader – thanks to them offering up their body – to personify its own historical strength. This is not about a leader projecting his individuality onto the people, but a people reactivating its historical strength through the body of the leader. In other words, the leader belongs to the people (and not the other way around). If the name of the leader becomes an inscription surface for various claims and antagonisms, this is precisely because it no longer belongs only to the person who embodies it. This allows us to realize that the leader does not manipulate and shape the "masses" to their every fancy and whim as an extension of their limitless enjoyment or private passions. Rather, on the contrary, the leader makes their body available for the construction of a popular historical force – i.e. a national-popular project.

We now arrive at the second point that we would like to work through in this essay: the problem of the national in terms of the national-popular, since this idea would seem to be tied to identitarianism and to represent an insurmountable barrier to building an internationalist project. To do so, therefore, we will attempt to explain better what we understand by "the national" and why we believe it should not be associated with identitarianism.

Toward an internationalist populism

There is a long tradition in Latin American debates that is not well known in Europe and the United States, and which clearly distinguishes between two ideas of the nation. The first of these is built "from above" by Latin American oligarchies. While coinciding with the emergence of independent republics, this idea of the nation internalizes all of the culturalist remnants of colonialism, promoting – despite its avowed cosmopolitan liberalism – the separation and isolation of peoples. This is, therefore, an idea of the nation that tends to invisibilize and impede the cultural and political production by oppressed subjects, reproducing the framework of colonial contempt for and the exclusion of the people from the construction of the national ethos. The second, on the other hand, is the idea of a nation constructed "from below," by those subjects historically excluded from the other national narrative. This idea inherits the entire imaginary of popular struggles and transformations that have unfolded from the conquest to the present day.

While the first idea of the nation received the name of nationalism (or the oligarchic nation), the second has instead been called the national-popular. However, there is a debate (that we discussed in Essay 3) between those who identify nationalism with the figure of the state and who therefore assume that any idea of the nation-state threatens and betrays the national-popular, and those of us, who, on the contrary, believe that these two national forces (the oligarchic and the popular) are capable of generating different state-forms. Thus, to this very day we can find an irresolvable tension between elitist and popular configurations of the nation-state.

This genealogy first emerges in Latin America with José Carlos Mariátegui's proposals in Peru in the 1920s (Mariátegui, 1971) and the early reception of Antonio Gramsci in Argentina, beginning in 1947.[10] Contemporaries who nevertheless missed the opportunity to get to know each other's most relevant intellectual work,[11] Mariátegui and Gramsci both understood that the emergence of the national-popular entailed the construction of a hegemonic project for popular emancipation in countries where the heterogeneity of the social meant the absence of a homogeneous political subject (the working class) or indigenous subject (a particular ethnic group). Thus, Mariátegui and Gramsci both knew that any social transformation must be connected to a motor force articulating the constitutive heterogeneity of the social and shaping it into a popular will. And that motor force could not be built outside the register of feeling – hence, the careful attention both thinkers gave to the old romantic problem of the link between politics and aesthetics.[12] It is no coincidence that both thinkers would work through the problem of the national-popular through the question of literature in peripheral countries.[13]

What is interesting about all this is that, for both thinkers, national-popular projects did not exclude the possibility of constituting internationalist solidarity among oppressed subjects – they were its condition of possibility. Or, in other words, it was the possibility of embracing their condition as oppressed that could awaken solidarity among those finding themselves in a similar situation. So, concrete struggles against local oppressions would give rise to a universal form of solidarity and emancipation. Even Mariátegui goes so far as to say that "[t]he boundaries between nationalism and internationalism are not yet well clarified," and that "[e]lements of one [nationalism or internationalism] sometimes intertwine, with elements of the other." Furthermore, he argued that "[e]vidence shows that national realities are not necessarily in conflict with international realities," but that the problem of the national arises from "[t]he inability to understand and acknowledge this second and higher reality [which] is a simple myopia, a functional limitation. Dated, mechanical forms of intelligence employed in former national perspectives are incapable of understanding the new, vast, complex international perspective. They reject and deny it because they cannot adapt to it." To which he adds: "nationalism is valid as a claim, but not as a negation" (2011 [1924]: 259–60). Therefore, it is local struggles for emancipation that, Mariátegui continues, "weave a dense network of international solidarity that prepares the future of humanity" (Mariátegui, 2010 [1923]: 240). These passages from Mariátegui allow us to corroborate the idea that, in contrast to reactionary or identitarian nationalisms, it is possible to discover affirmative (or national-popular) nationalisms capable of giving shape to a local subject that can contribute to universal emancipation. To borrow a term formulated by Colombian thinker José Figueroa, we are speaking of a situated universality, not a formal and abstract universalism that seeks to mold each of our cultures like a straitjacket, but rather a local creation that expresses, in its own concreteness, a possible future for humanity.[14]

While it's true that the tradition of populist thought is best recognized in its Gramscian legacy, it would not be a bad idea to begin to reclaim Mariátegui's work, since both traditions shape the historical field of inquiry through which we can understand the emergence of populist theory. This displacement allows us to grant the populist link between the leader and the people a broader temporal arc of Latin American debates, helping to further complicate the already problematic link between the national and the international. What should be emphasized here is that, if identitarian nationalisms promote identitarian closure and do not allow for heterogeneity, popular tradition instead sets out from that constitutive heterogeneity as an ineradicable element of the national-popular ethos. Rooted in an idea of the nation born from the injustice of exclusion, it carries within itself the secret of an openness toward the other, an openness that tends toward the inclusion of the excluded. Regarding the specific case of populism, critics therefore often confuse national causes – inherited from the national-popular – with the exclusionary nationalism characteristic of oligarchies. Either because populism refers to the nation-state or because it configures the people in relation to a leader, the vast majority of works on the subject have taken for granted that populism is incompatible with internationalism.

However, the lack of research on populism's international or transnational dimension (we use these interchangeably because, as we will show later, the distinction is problematic) has begun to improve, however slightly. We see proof of this incipient interest in the subject in two recently published articles – one from the team led by Yannis Stavrakakis, and the other from Luis Blengino.[15] As to the first, De Cleen, Moffitt, Panayotu, and Stavrakakis (2019) explore the notion of transnational populism through Laclau and Mouffe's discourse theory and a case study of the Democracy in Europe Movement 2025 (DiEM25). They propose two conceptual distinctions. On the one hand, they distinguish between populism and nationalism, believing that the key distinction lies in the basic structure determining each. While, in terms of spatial metaphors, nationalist discourse "consists of the horizontal in/out distinction between members and non-members of the nation," populist discourse "is structured around a vertical, down/up axis that refers to power, status, and hierarchical socio-cultural and/or socio-economic positioning" (De Cleen et al., 2019: 6–7).

On the other hand, they distinguish international populism from transnational populism. International populism is where populists represent peoples – in the plural – as (national) particularities that cooperate strategically and temporarily with respect to certain international affairs in a kind of "marriage of convenience" (as with the latest wave of Latin American populism when leaders sought to coordinate the creation of the Bank of the South, or groups within the European Parliament such as Europe of Freedom and Direct Democracy, and Europe of Nations and Freedom). These are "cases where populists relying on nation-based conceptions of 'the people' temporarily enter into alliances with other 'national' populists within an international setting" (De Cleen et al., 2019: 8). Transnational populism, by contrast, points toward building a people – in the singular – that transcends national borders and seeks to go beyond the conjunctural necessities and particularities of each separate people-nation. If international populism is still anchored in the people-nation, transnational populism aims to forge a transnational people that precisely transcends particular national locations. Transnational populism, moreover, always maintains the populist element of a dichotomizing discourse whereby a transnational people "is discursively constructed as a large powerless group through opposition to 'the elite' conceived as a small and illegitimately powerful group" (De Cleen et al., 2019: 8).

These authors argue that the DiEM25 represents – in the contemporary political context – the best example of transnational populism, thus defined. The key to DiEM25 lay in its strategy of establishing a transnational people. The authors describe how DiEM25 was born in response to the experience of SYRIZA's populism in Greece, and fundamentally how its capitulation to the "Troika"[16] – especially after the 2015 referendum – was an affront to democracy insofar as it exposed the anti-democratic structure of the European Union. Faced with the failure of populism on the national level, the authors argue that DiEM25 represents a transnational strategy for democratizing Europe, and that, from the beginning, it acquired the populist element of dichotomizing discourse by establishing an antagonistic frontier between the people – "those on the bottom" – and the elite. And its transnational character was also present from the beginning insofar as it sought to build a people beyond the national level to stand up to a "global elite" comprising supranational institutions, transnational corporations, etc. However, and despite this transnational commitment, the authors do not refrain from noting the inescapable presence of the national component. The equivalential chain of transnational populism anchored in the signifier "democracy" pushed DiEM25's discursive structure to bring together demands for the democratization of the European Union with demands for the restoration of popular sovereignty at the regional, national, and local levels. In any case, DiEM25 had to embrace this connection and uphold "transnational democracy as a condition for democracy on any of the lower levels" (De Cleen et al., 2019: 14).

From our perspective, this suggestive analysis fails to clarify two aspects: on the one hand, the place of the leader, which is key to any definition of populism, since, apart from mentioning Yanis Varoufakis, it tells us nothing about the place of the leader within a transnational populist articulation. On the other hand, the distinction between international populism and transnational populism becomes problematic at one point. If international populism entails merely bringing peoples together as national particularities defined as "those on the bottom," and transnational populism also implies the construction of a people from below, but one which "surpasses the boundaries of the nation-state," doesn't this approach somehow understand the universal as unmediated by particularities? Would this transnational people be a people uncontaminated by national particularities? In fact, in this case study, the authors note tensions within DiEM25 in this regard when they point out that "its move towards the transnational is not total, and the national remains crucial to its demands for democracy" (De

Cleen et al., 2019: 17). Perhaps the appearance of DiEM25 in national elections should be understood as proof that (national) particularities are ineradicable in the conformation of a transnational people.[17] In any case, Laclau and Mouffe's perspective helps us to see that such a "total" movement toward the transnational, completely detached from any national particularity, will always be impossible.

In the second text we mentioned at the outset of this section – that of Blengino – we find the opposite thesis – namely, that it is only through the affirmation of (national) particularities that a populist internationalism can be built. Hence the paradox that it is impossible to sustain an international populism without (populist) nationalisms. Luis Blengino (2019) arrives at this conclusion when he takes up Foucault and Laclau to make a counter-diagnosis of the present, where the transnational dimension of populism occupies a fundamental position. His text originates in opposition to Slavoj Žižek's diagnosis[18] of the present, in which he does not hesitate to criticize populism and to belittle recent populist experiences in South America. According to Žižek's diagnosis, the current contest between self-regulated financial globalization and the xenophobic neo-fascist reaction will result in a model of capitalism that is as efficient as it is authoritarian. This is the great threat that Latin American populisms were helpless against, since populism "is 'an opium of the people' at best, as in the case of Kirchnerism, and fascism at worst, i.e. 'a combination of left and right' with the goal of changing something so that nothing changes, as in Peronism" (Blengino, 2019). Against these arguments, Blengino proposes rescuing the geopolitical aspect of Foucault's history of governmentality, which is what is lacking in the theoretical-political wager of Laclau's populism. It is thus a question of adding the variable of anti-imperialism – understood as an abstract and imposing universalism – to make an accurate diagnosis of the times and to put into perspective the Latin American populist experiences that Žižek so confusedly mentions.

By introducing the variable of anti-imperialism, Blengino encourages us to distinguish between two types of populism:

populisms of the global core (which seek to maintain or reinforce a position of privilege within the world-system) and the anti-imperialist populisms of the global periphery (which seek to change their position within the world-system). This distinction, moreover, also corresponds to the dividing line between reactionary populisms – supported by nationalist and xenophobic authoritarianism – and emancipatory populisms, whose distinctive characteristic is their transnational dimension. Hence, for peripheral/emancipatory populisms, there is no possibility of successfully emerging from their antagonism with local oligarchies if they don't embrace the international context as their framework for struggle. The antagonism that peripheral/emancipatory populisms embody vis-à-vis local oligarchies may in principle appear simply in terms of internal politics, but it is necessarily linked to a struggle that transcends national borders, since it presumes "a problem of international politics, of confrontation with the power-structure of the world-system that local oligarchies rely upon" (Blengino, 2019).

With these theoretical elements in hand, Blengino shifts his argument toward Latin American cases, arguing that Peronist populism represents a counter-conduct movement, the main victim of the genocide perpetrated by the last military dictatorship that installed a neoliberal regime in Argentina.[19] Far from being accurately characterized as fascism – as Žižek so flippantly claims – Peronism is a populist, statist, and nationalist articulation, and is therefore at the same time necessarily internationalist. In any case, Blengino insists that it is a political formation anchored in a popular nationalism – not a xenophobic or racist nationalism – whose central discursive elements include the fight for political sovereignty, economic independence, and social justice, objectives that "cannot be achieved from the periphery of the world-system in isolation. That's why Peronist nationalism is essentially transnational. It is inseparable from regional integration and the articulation of peoples (through the singularity of every nation) and markets to stand up as a geopolitical region against the imperial regime of neoliberal globalization" (Blengino, 2019).

Thus, Blengino turns Žižek's own arguments against him. Žižek's defense of non-racist nationalism can be seen – very much despite his intentions – as the pillar of an internationalist populism, since it is "an authentic nationalism [that] consists precisely in admitting its own limits" (Blengino, 2019). The concrete Latin American experience of a decade of populism – with projects like the Union of South American Nations (UNASUR) or the Mercosur Parliament (PARLASUR) – took transnational populism from being a helpless utopia and gave it the status of a heterotopia. In any case, we can add that, aside from the neoliberal counter-reaction, this materialization of an alternative form of internationalism to neoliberal globalization cannot be taken as a failure. Although we disagree with the distinction that Blengino proposes between the two types of populism, we believe that the reflections he raises coincide with the historical field of inquiry pertaining to Latin American debates: between a (self-enclosed) oligarchic nation and an (open and internationalist) national-popular nation.

Now, what these two articles show – despite what we have shown to be their differences – is that populism, with its leaders and its peoples, can be perfectly compatible with a transnational project. The populist leader could only be thought of as an impediment if we understand them (wrongly, as we have already shown) to be a despotic narcissist, and the people could only represent an obstacle to the articulation of a transnational populism if it is taken to be a closed unit forged from an irreducibly identitarian principle. But if we maintain, on the one hand, that the people is an unstable articulation of demands that depends on its constitutive heterogeneity, and, on the other, that the leader is both responsible to the people and expresses the historical strength of that people, then other possibilities open up.

If those held responsible for the experience of a lack are the same among various "peoples," solidarity between demands can extend far beyond national boundaries. Hence, discursive dichotomization through the establishment of an antagonistic frontier between "those on the bottom" and "those on top" can slide beyond national boundaries, giving rise to an equivalence between peoples – an international populism. This is why the crises caused by neoliberal policies that led to the collapse of countries like Argentina in 2001, Bolivia from 2003 to 2005, and Ecuador in 2005, awakened internationalist solidarity to the point that those involved – on the basis of their own local demands – understood the various supranational organizations of neoliberalism, large corporations, and the United States government as the constitutive outside against which they needed to unify. This was the context that enabled the arrival of populist governments across Latin America, and their subsequent alliance that, among other things – at the Summit of the Americas in Mar del Plata, Argentina, in 2005 – defeated President George W. Bush's goal of imposing the Free Trade Area of the Americas (FTAA) and allowed for the creation of PARLASUR in 2005 and UNASUR in 2008.[20] Similarly, De Cleen et al. (2019) have shown how the equivalence of demands anchored in the signifier "democracy" has given rise in the European context – after what was interpreted as SYRIZA's surrender of the populist project in Greece – to the populism of DiEM25, whose stated objective is to build a transnational people.

Furthermore, what is interesting to note here is that transnationalism can be found throughout the political structures generated by alliances between populist governments and the formation of populist party structures that transcend national borders. But Latin America also shows that transnationalism can emerge on the level of popular organizations. We pointed out above that the people of populism is overflowing with organizations, and those organizations have often deployed their practices of solidarity on the transnational level. Let's take as examples the dissemination of the Cuban adult literacy method ("Yes I can") by way of various social, union, and political organizations; ongoing encounters between populist militants from different countries; and public demonstrations across different countries against attempted coups, and in support of the governments of Bolivia in 2008 and Ecuador in 2010. The same goes for leaders: Latin American populists have shown that leadership can transcend borders, not only in the massive events held by Hugo Chávez and Evo Morales in different countries across the region, but also in Dilma Rousseff's rallies outside Brazil to protest against the suspicious imprisonment of Lula and to reject Bolsonaro's fascism.

This is not exclusive to avowedly populist countries, since here we could add two emblematic cases led by women and taken up elsewhere for the building of popular power. On the one hand, the example of American Congresswoman Alexandria Ocasio-Cortez who, through the institutions, is proposing a Green New Deal in the face of the climate crisis that is leading to the worst forecasts worldwide in the coming decades. Through this pact, Ocasio-Cortez proposes rethinking existing productive relations, and the need to produce clean energy, from a popular and universalist perspective. The other example is that of Francia Márquez, a Colombian land activist (and winner of the Goldman Environmental Prize) who promotes a reconceptualization of the link between territory and the law. While this new link is understood through the struggles of black communities, it reflects something universal that disrupts the way that neoliberalism understands the relationship to territory, an extractive relation of control that tends to invisibilize the political and subjective construction of any territorial imaginary. Through these examples, then, we can conclude that it is local struggles, embodied in their leaders and articulated through the popular, that awaken ties of solidarity on the international level and promote new social bonds for contemplating alternative forms of humanity in the current crisis.

Essay 6
The Absent Cause of Populist Militancy

Post-foundationalism and the absence of guarantees

In the previous essay, we discussed in detail why the Freudian group or primal horde should not be confused with the people, and the decisive role that leadership plays in the construction of populism. We were able to establish how the leader – beyond whatever preponderance they might accrue – can never exist without a people, which in turn is only instituted through a process of organization. In other words, the emergence of the populist leader does not occur without the people and the people does not become such without the intervention of social movements, unions, political parties – *without militancy*.

In this section we are going to develop our reflections on populist militancy, understood as a new militant ethos suited to a post-foundational era.[1] The first question that arises is this: what does it mean to think about militancy in our present? It implies understanding, on the one hand, that our moment is organized according to a neoliberal ethos that seeks to consummate what Jorge Alemán has called "the perfect crime":[2] the construction of a subjective emplacement that seeks to reduce us to human capital by displacing *Homo politicus*, in order to definitively enthrone *Homo economicus*.[3] And, on the other hand, it means understanding that this epochal experience can no longer be reversed through the classic schemas of the left.[4] Here the question of emancipation that we have been addressing in previous essays returns from another angle. Ultimately, it is a question of thinking about how to build a militant emancipatory ethic when it is no longer possible to embrace the starting point of the traditional left, a subjective position built through an accumulation of certainties and inferences of meaning that became inevitable to us.

If it is no longer possible to begin from the premise that there exist certain foundations that determine a priori who is the primary protagonist of the emancipatory struggle and the legitimate dimensions that this struggle must contemplate, it becomes urgent to ask ourselves what logics can dictate militant actions. In turn, we are interested in showing that taking on the challenge of abandoning a position based on certain immovable foundational principles does not necessarily imply falling into the negative opposite and plunging into the most extreme anti-foundationalism. In other words, it is not necessary to assume a radical destruction of the world's foundations that would force us to succumb to the proposals of the most nihilistic or skeptical partisans of postmodernity. We therefore reject the subjective belief of postmodernism that "it's all the same," in which the assumption of a more radical relativism would lead us to think that "anything can be anything else." Or, in other words, we are interested in insisting that it is precisely in the acceptance of the lack of foundations and privileged subjects for change that the key to a new militant ethic lies.

Toward this end, it is possible to lay other foundations for a militant subjective position, since, once we have accepted the foundational character of the political (as we argued in Essay 1) and the idea of an interplay between the political and politics – which involves shaping reality as such – we find ourselves on the post-foundational terrain that we analyzed in Essay 1 through the contributions of Oliver Marchart

(2007, 2018). This means assuming, following Marchart, that we are not in the presence of a foundation in the sense of an essence underlying the existing order, which functions as an intelligibility principle capable of explaining the totality in a full, coherent, and clearly defined way. But nor are we faced with the absolute absence of some sort of bond that would prevent the establishment of any meaning, norms, or consistency. So we are faced with neither a foundation nor an anti-foundation, since we distance ourselves from both those positions that involve the idea of an absolute closure and those that presuppose a complete opening to the most radical relativism. Every order, every sedimented form of objectivity, totality, or subjectivity, is always politically constituted, precarious, and sutured insofar as it consists of networks of hegemonic relationships established through acts of institution.

The idea that we move on a post-foundational terrain can also be put in other terms – namely, that we move on the terrain of neither pure necessity nor pure contingency. Gloria Perelló, in an article entitled "Cause, Need, and Contingency: Some Political Implications" (2017), investigates from a psychoanalytic perspective the place of contingency, particularly in Ernesto Laclau's later writings, arguing that, in both Laclau and Lacan, contingency and necessity are not understood as opposites. On the contrary, they are understood in a type of relationship that breaks with the traditional opposition that establishes dualistic boundaries framing these concepts. Furthermore, she clarifies that neither author maintains the primacy of the logic of contingency over the logic of necessity. In any case, contingency cuts across necessity, so that to argue that it is no longer the logic of necessity that exclusively governs political action is not to say that political intervention is at the mercy of "pure" contingency. It is no longer a question of falling back onto these logics in their pure forms, but it is instead imperative to reconsider how they relate to one another. In our view, this is the terrain that allows us to begin to think about the implications of militant populist intervention.

Neither the cemetery nor the madhouse

Laclau liked to cite the words of Jorge Abelardo Ramos[5] – an Argentinean political leader alongside whom he had organized in his youth – who said that "society never polarizes between the madhouse and the cemetery."[6] This metaphor serves to illustrate the impossibility of inhabiting pure and completely opposite poles, and Laclau cited it to explain the impossibility of finding ourselves in a situation of pure reactivation or pure sedimentation, full antagonism or full institutionality, or of complete contingency or complete necessity. It is to the extent that we cannot establish an equilibrium between the two components of these binary pairs, a sort of continuum where the exact midpoint between two poles could be found (if this were the case, we would continue to be anchored in an understanding that accepts the possibility of fullness), that Laclau was forced to specify his concept of contingency.

Perelló (2017) reminds us that Laclau and Mouffe (1985) argued that contingency permeates the realm of necessity, and that the latter can no longer be understood as an underlying principle dictating the structuring of social identities. In discursive terms, this means understanding that there is no "literal" foundation that determines meaning within a system of relational differences, or, in social terms, that "necessity only exists as a partial effort to limit contingency" (Laclau and Mouffe, 1985: 114).[7] However, it is in a later text, *New Reflections on the Revolution of Our Time* (1990), that Laclau takes on the task of differentiating contingency from accident and chance. Perelló identifies a series of steps that Laclau deploys in his argument in order to establish this difference. In the first place, alongside Aristotle, Laclau distinguishes the essence of the accident. Second, with the support of arguments from Christianity, contingency gains a specificity within the general field of the accident. Third, Laclau arrives at his own concept of contingency – namely, as an experience linked to the limitation of being (in line with the definition he had presented alongside Mouffe in 1985, of antagonism as the limit of all objectivity). And fourth, he radicalizes his notion of antagonism by introducing the idea of dislocation.

If we briefly develop Laclau's (1990) arguments, we find that, in the first instance, he maintains that contingency is not equivalent to accident, but that it instead possesses a specificity within the general field of accidentality.[8] According to classical philosophy, there are no necessary causal determinations for the accident, but chance intervenes in an indeterminate way. Hence, the accident, given its indeterminacy, is not part of being – i.e. it cannot be integrated into being since being is necessary, determinate, and knowable. While the rational apprehension of the object implies grasping its essence, the accident, on the other hand, corresponds to something indeterminate and unknowable in the object.

Second, Laclau finds in Christianity a treatment of the accident that leads him to delimit the idea of contingency within the more general field of accidentality. In the presence of the Christian God – the only necessary being, in which contingency and necessity coincide – all other beings, products of *ex nihilo* creation by the almighty divinity, are contingent and finite. They are contingent because that is how beings "whose essence does not entail its existence" are defined (Laclau, 1990: 19), and contingency thus comes to refer to an existence that does not find in itself the principle of its necessity. They are finite because they exist at an immeasurable distance from their creator and are "susceptible to a radical annihilation and essentially vulnerable as a result. The identity of finite beings is a threatened identity. In this way, a dimension of negativity penetrates and is latent in any objectivity" (Laclau, 1990: 19).

In this way, and with the argument in hand that negativity permeates all objectivity, Laclau takes his third argumentative step to maintain that, unlike mere accident, contingency is linked to the experience of the limitation of being. Thus, from his perspective, this established that the social does not have a positive and objective character, since contingency – which is a sort of negativity – is constitutive of objectivity. Translated to the socio-political level: contingency implies that a social identity can only be constituted on the basis of an antagonistic force – which threatens and affirms it at the same time – not through determinations that are necessary in relation to a totality, and thus antagonism reveals the contingent and limited character of all identity. In any case, antagonism as the condition of existence for a totality refers to "[t]his link between the blocking and simultaneous affirmation of an identity [that] we call 'contingency,' which introduces an element of radical undecidability into the structure of objectivity" (Laclau, 1990: 21).

Finally, he introduces the notion of dislocation. Laclau insists that every being is dislocated in itself, since it is traversed by a constitutive gap that prevents it from closing in on itself as a full sameness. In other words, structural dislocation is the lack that enables the irruption of that not contemplated by the given order of possibilities, thereby forcing us to be free: "I am *condemned* to be free, not because I have no structural identity as the existentialists assert, but because I have *failed* structural identity" (Laclau, 1990: 44). He establishes dislocation as the *place of the subject* because it is the moment of decision beyond structural determinations, a contingent decision made on the basis of an undecidable structure. This entails a radicalization of the notion of antagonism, insofar as, as a function of dislocation, it was established as a way of "making something" from the irruption of the subject opened up by that same structural lack – or, put differently, antagonism is the form that "makes" what arises from dislocation into a political matter.

With these elements in hand, Perelló (2017) connects them to the distinction between *tuché* and *automaton* raised by Lacan in his exploration of accidental causes in Aristotle.[9] She tells us that Lacan presents the tuché and automaton as two accidental forms of repetition (two forms of repetition as effects of non-necessary causes). The automaton refers to the automatic functioning of the chain of signifiers without the intervention of the subject, understood as that which does not stop writing itself wrongly. The tuché, on the other hand, alludes to the encounter with the real, that which has no place within the web of signification, the unassimilable of trauma. While we can refer the automaton back to chance – without the intervention of the subject – the tuché, translated as fortune (or misfortune), cannot be associated with pure chance since it exists on the order of an encounter, the encounter of chance with the intention of the subject or, in other words, the moment of *decision on an undecidable terrain*. So, contingency should be understood through the tuché, and not through the automaton.

This is how Perelló (2017) argues that contingency – on the socio-political terrain – implies that a socio-political subjectivity is not constituted by necessary or automatic determinations in relation to a totality, but through the contingency that results from an *encounter between chance and the subject's decision on an undecidable terrain*. Obviously, understood in this way, the socio-political subjectivity that arises from that encounter will not be determined by the structure of already available options, nor will it be an *ex nihilo* creation, the absolute indeterminacy of a pure and complete foundational act. Rather, the socio-political subjectivity that emerges from that encounter will be an antagonistic response to the experience of a lack, beyond structural determinations but falling short of radical indeterminacy.

We have paused to think through the nature of contingency because it gives us a standard for understanding what constitutes a difference, what antagonism consists of, and when a reactivation becomes politicized. It is only when what is reactivated gains an antagonistic character that the political subjectivity that is constituted has the possibility of eliminating the status quo. Therefore, it can sometimes be the case that a moment of reactivation is converted into pure accident or mere chance insofar as it does not give shape to anything on the order of the political. This can occur because no antagonism is constituted and, ultimately, no subjectivity is forged that is capable of initiating a political struggle to transform the sedimented order. Since it may well happen that what emerges from dislocation is not experienced as a lack and not registered as an antagonism, but simply passes, fades away – is understood, for example, as mere fate, or attributed to natural causes or divine will. Something very different happens, on the other hand, if that moment of reactivation meets intentionality, a subjective intervention that forges an antagonism and gives rise to a political subjectivity, a militant task seeking to antagonistically shake up the sedimented order.

While we follow Marchart (2007, 2018) when he says that this is always a question of partial foundations, a constant process of foundation and de-foundation, we find it necessary to complement this with Perelló's arguments (2017), since that constant interplay of foundation and de-foundation is governed neither by accident nor by chance, but by the contingency that results from the intersection of chance and intentionality – i.e. from the moment of decision on an undecidable terrain. It is here that we argue that populism, leadership, and *militancy* come into play. A new type of militancy means that those who are willing to engage in antagonistic struggles are alert to structural dislocation, i.e. that chance finds them prepared for the subject to emerge, available to be traversed by contingency, which interrupts impossibility precisely insofar as it pushes the limits of the possible. Populist militancy means going beyond the merely programmatic; it means taking responsibility for the incalculable; it means, quite simply, being guided by an (emancipatory) desire with no guarantees. A popular revolt can lead to an emancipatory outcome, but it can also end in reactionary closure. The lack of guarantees thus demands this type of militancy since it would be difficult for the sedimentation that follows from a moment of reactivation to gain an emancipatory tenor without this kind of militant subjective position. The outcome of an antagonistic struggle could imply victory or defeat for militant political struggle, but the status quo could hardly be transformed in an emancipatory direction without that struggle.

Let's take two examples, the first being the reactivation of sedimented practices that brought about the "cycle of rebellion"[10] in Bolivia between 2000 and 2005. The first question we can ask is whether this social transformation would have taken place without the intervention and synergy

of the leadership of Evo Morales with the militant organizations of coca farmers, when Morales' famous phrase "Now is
the Time" became a political rallying-cry and precipitated the
antagonistic struggle in moments that shook the neoliberal
status quo. Our answer is no. It was precisely the intentionality of the coca farmers' antagonistic struggle that made the
difference. The other example is Spain's 15-M Movement,
which emerged in 2011,[11] and which many understand as
a moment of reactivation without intentionality. But it was
not until the emergence of Podemos that this experience
configured a political subjectivity and a militant task that
allowed the movement to take the next step beyond the
merely reactive moment of rejecting the austerity policies
of Mariano Rajoy's Popular Party government. Podemos
introduced a hitherto absent militant ethic that transformed
Spain's political order – no one in the political sphere
emerged unscathed by Podemos' intervention.

Locating ourselves in the post-foundational field implies
assuming the subjective responsibility of a militancy toward
the real nucleus of impossibility. This encapsulates the
militant questions that we will address in what follows.

The three militant questions

The differences between the experiences of Bolivia's Movement
for Socialism (MAS)[12] and Podemos help us to shift toward a
first problematic aspect of militancy. As we mentioned above,
the Bolivian experience was shaped from the beginning by a
synergy between popular organizing and the leadership of
Evo Morales. The Spanish experience, by contrast, witnessed
other nuances, since the 15-M was born first and Podemos
leadership – in the figure of Pablo Iglesias – only emerged
later. All of which refers us to the debate about the instituent
practices that should (or should not) follow a moment of
reactivation.

Podemos was the instituted expression of the instituent
irruption of 15-M. At a time when Podemos seems to have
entered into an irreversible process of liquefaction, many

scholars attempting to explain the causes of this failure long for that moment of instituent enthusiasm, as though some original purity had been betrayed by the subsequent institutional creation. Here, then, we find some leverage for those intensifying criticisms that argue that any attempt to institutionally translate a moment of reactivation means from the outset its capture and perversion by the force of routine in the already instituted field. We refer to those who reject a priori any hegemonic attempt to build a people and seek to remain faithful to an idea of the event; those who see in any instituted experience a betrayal of the instituent moment; those who see parliamentary representation, access to executive power, or any link with state logics as unfaithful to the instituent act of the multitude.

Obviously, the latter are susceptible to easy condemnation due to the mere fact that no attempt at institutionalization can fully absorb the moment of reactivation. And we should also bear in mind that, while the moment of reactivation is attractive due to its temporal dislocation that calls into question sedimented practices, suspends routines, and thus entails a disassociation from certain positions, militant intervention that seeks to account for that reactivation, by contrast, entails the discomfort, disappointment, and displeasure brought on by the reframing that attempting to remain inevitably causes.[13] A political subjectivity that seeks to embrace reactivation will involve initiating antagonisms, creating frontier effects, routinizing practices, and generating forms of institutionalization that – despite our best efforts – will always fail in their attempt to perfectly contain the moment of reactivation. However, the paradox that arises here is that, without this second moment of institutionalizing effort, we cannot create new sedimented practices or give any (emancipatory) meaning to the moment of reactivation. And this is the same paradox that traverses militancy: how to achieve a form of institutionalization that can accommodate the moment of reactivation? Or, put another way: how can we ensure that the routinization of militant practices does not block the emergence of the subject? The answer lies in a type of militancy that is cognizant of the fact that there is no form of institutionalization – whether a political party, social movement, union, circle,[14] etc. – that can resolve the moment of reactivation once and for all. If we do not embrace this kind of subjective position, militancy runs the risk of domesticating everything that is new and reducing it to organizational logic.

If we return to the example of Podemos, we see that, once the populist hypothesis proposed by Íñigo Errejón – the party's number 2 – had been abandoned, the narrative of the trenches developed, bringing with it an identitarian retreat that conflated the moment of reactivation with an organizational logic. Pablo Iglesias embraced this discourse after his break with Errejón, and in light of the need to give the party he was leading a political orientation. Thus, he opted for a quick reading of Gramsci's concept of trench warfare to adopt a position of retreat to within civil society, and to define "the working class" as the subject his party represented. He thereby determined the identity of his militants and, having secured that nucleus that did not question his militant leadership, he began the phase of pacts and negotiations to occupy quotas of power within the institutions. This entailed two things. On the one hand, it consolidated the idea of a previously determined political subject, thereby reactivating all the imagery associated with conventional forms of class struggle. And, on the other hand, all protest against this recourse to identitarianism and posing reactivation through difference was deactivated and its participants expelled from the movement through a discretionary measure that pulled them out from the roots. In other words, the moment of political negotiation that allowed for maintaining differences while building the people was blocked. So, instead of letting tensions live and seeking the path of political negotiation, Podemos embraced the classic logic of the left – namely, to embrace a predetermined subject and cause, and to expel anyone putting these at risk.

It is here that the advantage of populist militancy might lie: insofar as it is not established a priori or ever fully determined who can be part of the people, what its institutional forms should be, the dimensions that the antagonistic struggle should take, or who its enemies should be, etc., it always has the possibility of trying to keep something of that moment of reactivation alive. The people, by not being something given, functions as a precarious articulation of equivalences that requires both organization and reactivation at the same time. In other words, while it requires a structure to guide its militant practices, to offer arguments to support its positions in debates, and to establish lines of political action, the people is never a finished subject, it is not the result of an arithmetic sum or the product of an electoral majority, and it is not reducible to a sociologically determined group. The people is a contingent political construct that is not always present, and therefore, if populist militancy is to keep it alive once it has emerged, it can never block the irruption of the subject (or the moment of reactivation).

When we argue that radical contingency implies traversing necessity, we return to the idea that sedimentation never manages to fully domesticate reactivation and, vice versa, that reactivation never means the complete *tabula rasa* elimination of sedimented practices. Every political intervention – no matter how radically innovative – always takes place on an established hegemonic terrain. And here we find another problem that populist militancy faces: it operates from the outset on enemy terrain. Thus, while populist militancy confronts the challenge of maintaining openness within its organizations, it also simultaneously collides with and embodies its antagonisms in a discursive field established by neoliberalism. The question at this point is: could this possibly be different? From our perspective, the answer is no. But this is precisely what is so often neglected by those who criticize populist experiences, rejecting them through the accusation that, in practice, they take refuge in capitalist parliamentarism, reinforce the neoliberal subjectivity of a class of consumers and/or debtors (who ultimately end up becoming their gravediggers), or reproduce a form of capitalism that is unable to transform the extractivist matrix.[15] When we say that no intervention takes place as a pure act that creates something new and uncontaminated, we are ultimately saying that any irruption of the subject and new subjectivity thereby created intervenes on already partially sedimented terrain. Hence, also, the tension between its antagonistic power and its limits, because what would it be like to intervene politically from a pure and uncontaminated exteriority?

In turn, although it embodies antagonisms within a discursive field imposed by the enemy, we can nevertheless insist that the people and its militants represent an excess that becomes unassimilable, because populism by definition overflows certain nodal points of neoliberal subjectivity. If the populist gesture is a collective, egalitarian, political excess, then it contradicts the logic of the *Homo economicus* of human capital (Brown, 2017). The people and its militancy have equality inscribed in their very form, an egalitarian excess that subverts neoliberal norms of meritocracy, the difference between winners and losers, and the inequality that competition between human capital entails. The people and its militancy also imply a collective excess because they presuppose a bond with the other that transcends the isolated, individual responsibility of the entrepreneur-of-the-self in which neoliberal rationality traps us. It is worth mentioning that, in moments like these, the people and its militancy interrupt the solipsistic enjoyment that neoliberal capitalism proposes.

The people and its militancy also carry the political in their own emergence. They stage politics and make it newly thinkable by bringing it up to date through mobilizations, assemblies, the occupation of various spaces (streets, squares, factories, universities, etc.), thereby relaunching the public over the private, the collective over the individual, and destabilizing the neoliberal attempt to cancel *Homo politicus* by recapturing the exercise of popular sovereignty. In this sense, we can say that the people and populist militancy in the neoliberal context revive the duality that Bataille (1985 [1933]) found in the nature of the sovereign. A sovereign is not only the one who exercises the power to dominate, it is also the one who stands up as radically other in the face of the homogenizing forces of the social order – be it the useless, the incalculable, or the immeasurable.[16] Hence, against the homogenizing onslaught of neoliberal subjectivity, the emancipatory opening of untameable and unconquerable popular excess arises.

Finally, let's return to the antagonisms that militants embody: can we say – for the reasons explained above – that the emancipatory power of the people boils down to militancy? The answer is still paradoxical: the people implies the simultaneous experience of emancipatory possibility and impossibility. If it is a matter of understanding emancipation in singular and unilateral terms, as a future horizon that is accomplished once and for all, then this is impossible. But this impossibility does not prevent militant struggle for partial and plural emancipations. If, according to the classical left, militant actions were directed by a principle of determination, as a necessary cause, and with an objective that was also defined a priori, from a post-foundational perspective, on the other hand, populist militancy can be understood through the idea of the "absent cause."

Let's turn to the arguments developed by Biglieri and Perelló in their book *The Uses of Psychoanalysis in Ernesto Laclau's Theory of Hegemony* (2012), and discuss the Lacanian concept of "absent cause" in its double-sense. An absent cause is, on the one hand, a cause that must be defended or a cause that must be won, and, on the other hand, a cause as a principle or foundation that produces effects.[17] In the first case, when a cause is taken up as something to defend or to win, it will always be a failure since it can never be fully realized as such. And, in the second case, when the cause is understood as a principle or a foundation, it will always be a lost cause insofar as it is absent. Contrary to what academic or scientific knowledge suggests – i.e. that, if the cause is removed, its effects disappear – in the case of the lost cause, we hold that there are effects precisely because these effects only occur in the absence of the cause – that is, we are dealing with an absent cause. In this way, the double-sense of the absent or lost cause means that we have neither starting points nor finish lines, because there are no foundations from which to begin or derive ultimate meaning, nor objectives established a priori to be fully achieved.

The "lost cause" – as a function of the impossible – does not imply helplessness, paralysis, or resignation, but is instead an experience that aims "to turn the absent foundation into a cause" (Alemán, 2009: 14). In any case, in the presence of the "lost cause," something will always be lacking, something will always be in excess – in other words, there will always be an insistent "real": "What doesn't stop not being written" (Lacan, 1999 [1972–3]: 59). Finally, this implies being aware that it is the lack of guarantees that evokes a militant call to get involved in political struggles. It calls on us to adopt an ethical position because, since nothing is guaranteed in advance, since we don't know what results political struggles can produce, and since there is no guarantee that the rights we have won today will continue to exist tomorrow, we must become militants. It is the militant call from the impossible that prevents us from sinking into the resignation of helplessness and urges us to adopt the subjective responsibility of building a people *against* the neoliberal night.

Essay 7
We Populists are Feminists

Let's imagine the future

It is very difficult today to regain our enthusiasm for images of a world that doesn't yet exist. Our reference points for emancipations to come are completely shot through with our past, and more precisely with those imaginaries that have shaped the idea of who we are today. But we often forget to problematize what kind of relationship we want to establish with a past that promised emancipation and that demarcates the political forms of our contemporary sensibility. We tend to reproduce an overly spontaneist relationship that swings back and forth from enthusiasm to failure, in a vicious oscillation between the nostalgic vindication of worn-out images and the sudden disenchantment of the impossibility of returning to them. Furthermore, it seems that this sponta-neist circularity ends up being complicit with the neoliberal ethos, as if it were cultivating our sensory intelligence to the point of leaving it trapped in a total immobility that forecloses on any idea of the future. Isn't the most sponta-neous and paradoxically durable image of our present precisely the absence of a future? Beyond this lack of imagi-nation, we even find with bewilderment that the reactionary powers of the present have managed to recycle those same emancipatory images, turning them into affective pastiches and mobilizing popular sectors toward their own reactionary ends. All this leads us to wonder whether we have forgotten how to imagine the future, or whether we are witnessing a still undeciphered transformation in our relationship with the past, with images, and with our sensibility. This question is not about evading reality, but instead getting right to the heart of the existing, i.e. pointing to a series of images from the past or signs that, forging against the conventional ethos of the left, help us to connect differently to our canceled futures.

Along these lines, it seems to us that both the figure of the feminine (that has been problematized, reappropriated, and interrogated by feminist struggles)[1] and the figure of the popular (constructed through populism) can give us clues for imagining that which does not yet exist.[2] Thus, we echo Nancy Fraser's warning, in her prologue to A Feminism of the 99% (2018), that "feminism is just one social movement, and needs to coordinate its claims and proposals with the rest of the movements, which should also move in the direction of 99%. We should not forcibly insist that the feminist movement is the privileged position for political action or the new historical subject of emancipation. Feminism is essential, but it has to be part of something bigger, an even broader political project" (Fraser, 2018: xii). But we also agree with what black feminism has been warning for several years, fully aware of the need to connect different emancipatory struggles capable of breaking the oppressions of class, race, and gender at the same time (Carneiro, 2000; Curiel, 2016). On the other hand, we are indebted to a certain tradition of Latin American feminism that has been thinking about the need to reconnect militancy, the popular field and the possibility of an anti-neoliberal feminist state (Álvarez, 1998; Gargallo, 2006; Femenías, 2007; Carosio, 2009; Matos and Paradis, 2013; Rivera Berruz, 2018). But it seems that, when we try to theorize feminism alongside populism, something collides, since it is difficult to imagine them together as part of the same political struggle, creating a rift that weakens the emancipatory force of both parts (Cadahia, 2019).

If we wonder about the missed encounters between feminism and populism, it seems to us that, in the case of feminism, this rejection comes from certain feminist traditions in both Latin America (autonomist, communitarian, and/or Spinozist feminisms)[3] and Europe (feminisms grounded in theories of difference)[4] that expel antagonism (and therefore negativity) when it comes to forging their own political project.[5] In fact, in her most recent book *Feminist International* (2020: 200), Verónica Gago counterposes populist articulation to feminist dynamics and assumes that "feminist struggles present an anti-neoliberal perspective capable of going beyond populist political articulation." In order to sustain this opposition, Gago identifies feminist struggles with the true autonomy of grassroots assembly dynamics and grants these an affirmative and expansive power [as *potencia*] that would overflow the articulatory ambitions of populist theory. Furthermore, she identifies assemblies with the popular-community level, in order to contrast these with what she understands as the popular-abstract framework of populism, and to critique the latter from within the feminist tradition.[6]

In the case of populism, on the other hand, the problem lies in certain barriers to theorizing the feminization of the popular[7] and the role of the political category of care in the construction of the people.[8] In other words, this is a question of the difficulties that the popular field often confronts when it relegates feminist demands to being a second-order problem. Or, in terms of the problem of care: when priority is given to the contradictions between the social production of value (labor) and capital, and the types of exploitation generated by the contradiction between the social reproduction of life (care) and capital are omitted. But what happens if, instead of widening the gap between feminism and populism – as Gago's text would seem to do – we instead try to dissolve this disagreement and begin to explore a link between antagonism and care?

Now, before developing our hypotheses on this disagreement and offering a possible alternative connection, we would like to explain a bit better what we are going to focus on to carry out this task. To do so, we would like to delve into the sensory dimension, or the role that sense plays in the construction of these two simultaneously theoretical and practical approaches. For this, we would like to assemble some ideas from Carlo Ginzburg (2013) that can help us to foster a perhaps underexplored disposition toward images that, following Ginzburg, we would like to call the *evidential paradigm*. According to Ginzburg, the evidential paradigm is a vestige of ancient hunting practices like reading footprints, a practice that has allowed for the building of all narration and configuration of meaning on the basis of the absent prey (or thing). As an illustration of this practice, Ginzburg turns to the old eastern fable *Zadig*, since it tells the story of three brothers who are able to reconstruct, through a series of clues, an animal they had never seen: the camel. Thus, the evidential paradigm is sustained on the basis of something that, since it cannot be experienced directly, strangely requires the exercise of our sensibility and intelligence to put the imagination to work. Ginzburg adds that this evidential exercise allows us to construct rhetorical images or figures that we cannot find delimited in the sedimented space of social reality, such that "the fact that the rhetorical figures on which the language of venatic deduction still rest ... are traceable to the narrative axis of metonymy" (Ginzburg, 2013: 93).

Unlike the positivist paradigm, which assumes that things are what they are and each object coincides with itself in a game of truth by correspondence, the evidential paradigm seems to suggest that things are not what they are since the thing cannot coincide with itself. So, in his text, Ginzburg goes on to identify this paradigm with the ancestral medical knowledge of body reading, Sherlock Holmes detective novels, Freudian psychoanalysis, and, in a certain sense, Morelli's study of art history – disciplines or practices whose object of knowledge escapes the mechanism of conventional representation. We can only refer to the thing through its effects: its symptoms, evidence, and footprints. Recall that this paradigm functions as a way of knowing from the place of not-knowing, from conjectural knowledge. In other words, it is experienced through clues that allow for the articulation of affects and intelligence in the very production of knowledge. Ginzburg not only identifies this knowledge with disciplines of formal knowledge, however, but goes on to say that the evidential paradigm "can be found throughout the entire world, with no limits of geography, history, ethnicity, sex, or class … it is the property of … hunters; of sailors; of women. It binds the human animal closely to other animal species" (Ginzburg, 2013: 113). Through this quote, we can see that he is referring to a conjectural, plebeian knowledge that neither seeks nor offers a finished picture of reality – one based on the sensory experience that sets different planes of what we have come to call the human into motion.

But we can also see that there is something plebeian and feminine[9] operating in this form of knowledge, a way of inhabiting not knowing, conjecture, and uncertainty that fosters a series of sensory connections still to be explored in all their radicalism. Furthermore, perhaps the question to which Ginzburg's entire proposal points, and which he seems to demarcate without fully explaining, is the following: what kind of rigor – understood as a form of decipherment that makes an opening toward the future legible – does this form of thinking historically associated with the feminine and plebeian suggest? Regardless, continuing to explore this possibility means taking up, as noted above, a series of theoretical difficulties in linking the feminine to the popular in a populist key, as if the problems of feminism were on one side and those of populism on the other. Therefore, in order to promote an articulation between both traditions, it seems essential to do two things. On the one hand, to ask ourselves whether it is possible to embrace antagonism through post-Marxist feminism,[10] and, on the other, to ask whether it is feasible to discover a form of care within populism. We believe that the basis of this missed encounter can be found in feminist claims that block antagonism (and negativity), and populist proposals that deny the role of care and the feminization of politics.

Feminism without identitarian closure

For some time now, an interesting political debate has been emerging about the need to *feminize politics through the sphere of care* (Carosio, 2009).[11] Along these lines, it would be useful not only to ask ourselves about the connection between this new locus of political enunciation and the survival of Ginzburg's plebeian evidential paradigm, but also to investigate where the irruption of this locus leads us – i.e. how it helps us to decipher the popular field. For this reason, we need to think more precisely about the scope of this demand, and to examine more carefully the drive to close conflicts, and the meaning that lay behind this possibility. Seen this way, there is a danger of turning the feminization of politics into an ethic of care that, by politicizing what has historically been called "domestic," runs the risk of turning the "domestic" – the sphere of reproduction of social life – into the only possible horizon of the political. At the same time, this would seem to emphasize a non-conflictual form of politics, as if conflict and rupture fall on the masculine side, and reconciliation and closure of antagonisms fall broadly on the feminine side. Doesn't the search for an affirmation of one's existence without taking on the negativity of confronting what we oppose run the risk of killing politics and thereby blocking the meaning that this unique form of emancipatory struggle brought about? Is it possible to formulate an idea of care that incorporates populist antagonism?

We believe that to do so we need to interrogate three assumptions that are found, on the one hand, at the heart of the communitarian perspective of some Latin American feminisms, and, on the other, in the ontological wager that authors like Gago deploy to read new feminist dynamics in terms of an affirmative power that expands from within itself without the need for negativity (antagonisms).[12] These assumptions are: autonomism, the illusion of immediacy, and the belief in corporeality as the opposite of power.[13] Regarding the first point, there is a belief that any appeal to the state or representational forms serves as a mechanism for co-opting the immanence of emancipatory struggles, making necessary the practice of self-management without any institutional or representative mechanism. The second point, which is associated with the first, consists of believing that certain locations exist prior to any articulation, places that owe their existence only to themselves and that, therefore, enjoy a privileged role in social transformation. In turn, by virtue of not being articulated through classic forms of politics, these locations are positioned as the opposite of power. Finally, this location prior to any articulation and free from state co-optation is none other than the body and the affects, as expressed through their multiple affirmative differences (without constitutive negativity), and any attempt to articulate these within a unity would merely ensnare them in the traps of power.

In this sense, it is important to note that the question of care tied to this philosophy of affirmative power brings to light an old problem of modern philosophy – namely, the problem of community. Recall that the emergence of the figure of the individual – understood as a disintegrating force vis-à-vis the undifferentiated unity of the community – generated a classic tension between individual freedom and the dissolution of the social fabric, which translated into a threat of disintegration for the community. Faced with this, different kinds of responses emerged that oscillated between nostalgia for a lost unity, attempts to rebuild it, acceptance of the era of individualism, and a transformation of the meaning of that community.

We could say that the contemporary translation of this problem seems to be understood as an unconfessed gender dichotomy: namely, the feminine as the locus for the recovery of communal meaning and the possibility of life in common – through care or the affective and expansive bringing together of bodies – and the masculine as the disaggregating element, through the perpetuation of antagonism, power, and the hierarchy of the social. The major drawback of approaching care through the perspective of the assembly (Gago, 2020) or the community (Rivera Cusicanqui, 2018) rests on the fact that this affirmative expansion – immanently from itself and for itself – does not explain how these articulations are produced, or to what extent they are indebted to the internal conflict that organizes them, and, above all, shows a lack of solidarity and political imagination toward other instances of political struggle. It is as if they repeat the *naïveté* of believing in privileged subjects of emancipation and that some forms of political struggle are outmoded – as if unions or the state were mere vestiges of the past – and, most complicatedly, that the contamination of their struggles by other subjects or cases would be detrimental to true emancipation. Doesn't this run the risk of assuming the completeness of a subject – feminism – which jeopardizes the indeterminacy and lack of guarantees characteristic of political militancy?

Faced with this, it seems to us that the task is not so much to discover privileged locations (or subjects) of social transformation but, instead, following Fraser, to reinvent in political praxis the distinction between the reproduction (care) of life and the production (labor) of social value, without sacrificing either the emancipatory horizon or the social protection that a populist and feminist reading of institutions can offer (Fraser, 2016: 117). In our opinion, the problem does not lie in the idea of care itself but in the autonomist matrix – in both its communitarianism and its affirmative ontology – through which this question has been theorized. In this sense, it seems possible to reflect on the political role of care through a different matrix that takes antagonism as its starting point and does not assume the politicization of the domestic or communal as the only possible horizon for the political. To do so, the notion of perseverance proposed by Joan Copjec, and the ethics of the not-all raised from the Lacanian left by authors like Jorge Alemán, can help us give shape to this connection.

In her book *Imagine There's No Woman* (2002), Copjec distinguishes between two types of drives: fixation and perseverance. She explores these drives through the tragic figures of Creon and Antigone, identifying the former with fixation and the latter with perseverance. The first drive takes place out of the belief that a totality – or a lost object – can be restored. In turn, the satisfaction experienced by working on the thing depends on an idea of the good that organizes actions from the outside and prescribes the form of enjoyment. In other words, Creon believes that there is an idea of the good to follow (the thing seen from the outside) that can be embodied in the figure of the state and preemptively delimited by an identification between his discourse and the law. This sets out from the idea that action comes to fulfill an end (the idea of the good) and that the actions of the state – insofar as they follow this idea – will be able to restore a lost identity (the fullness of the community). The problem, Copjec warns us, is that since "the thing" cannot be restored, since the idealization of the good collides with the reality of our drives, the responsibility for that lack of closure is placed on another (Antigone).

Thus, enjoyment comes to be structured as a *plus* that is achieved between the idealization of the demand and what is actually obtained, i.e. through the difference that organizes my action in terms of a dissatisfaction experienced between the idea of the good and the reality of things. Thus, Creon is "driven by an idealization of the difference between the satisfaction demanded and that which can be achieved through work" (Copjec, 2002: 46). That is to say, he is driven by a superego (the idea of the good) that maintains him in a constant state of dissatisfaction, and his fixation revolves around the fact that something has been lost due to the appearance of Antigone (the feminine) on the scene. In other words, he becomes obsessed and works toward the idea of preserving the state – protecting the public thing (*res publica*) from Antigone – which makes his fixation coincide with the lost thing with which it identifies. Such is his obsession that it makes him indifferent to "available objects" – i.e. everything that seems to violate his idealization of the state.

Antigone's work around her desire, by contrast, "is driven by the satisfaction afforded by her love for her brother, which provides the pressure or tension necessary to act" (Copjec, 2002: 46), and it is this action in relation to her drive that is given the name *perseverance*. Here, action is not stimulated by the idealization of and fixation on the good, but by a loving bond that is built through desire and determines the autonomy of action and the possibility of short-circuiting unequal dependence on the field of the other – the locus of masculine enunciation. So it is through perseverance that we open ourselves up to "acting in conformity with the real of desire" (Copjec, 2002: 45), without first projecting an idea of the good that should govern the subject.

With Copjec, we can affirm that Creon *identifies* with the public Thing and believes that he can exhaust with his own voice everything that it has to tell us. By having faith in his *exclusive path* into public life, he became convinced of his *exclusive right* to the Thing itself and trusted that it would only be expressed through a masculine voice. But the thing (thus fixed) is only a fossil – it has nothing to tell us aside from the empty echo of what has been self-expressed unilaterally (and naturalized) as a masculine voice. If we absolve the Thing from itself and identify with it, the thing itself would be dead. Unlike Creon, Antigone does not identify with the Thing because she knows that it is irreplaceable – her brother is what he is. At most, she dares to *say* that thing publicly, to tell the public that there is something irreducible (in law, in the state, in public life) that cannot be replaced by the very act of naming it. As an action, perseverance protects us from identifying our voice with the law, on both the masculine and feminine sides. After all, Antigone represents a movement that points beyond our fixations and preserves, from within the storage chest of our desires, that which cannot be substituted – but only sublimated.

What is interesting here is that, while the drive of fixation antagonizes through the belief that there is a good to follow, assuming that the political is articulated from the outside and through an idea of the law, the drive of perseverance antagonizes through the need to construct a loving bond, a way of building the common through the irreducible. On the terrain of the feminization of politics and the breach that places the masculine and the feminine into tension with one another, if we totalize the masculine as something to be eradicated through the feminine, with the feminine speaking from itself and for itself, we would be fixed into the same masculine procedure as Creon – namely, the masculine as that totality that comes to be destroyed by my totalized exceptionality: a double-totalization that is now being built from the opposite pole of those who have been historically oppressed. On the other hand, if we understand antagonism through the drive of perseverance, the feminization of politics can be associated with the construction of an antagonism through a de-totalized loving bond. In this direction, the ethic of the not-all is the possibility of thinking about feminism as a disruption of the logic of the totality, short-circuiting the biologization of the feminine and masculine as man and woman.

This logic, inherited from psychoanalysis, and which has come to be called the not-all, embraces the indeterminacy of reality – the non-existence of previously constituted identities – as the starting point for thought, while understanding the ontological dimension of the feminine and the masculine without reducing these to the factical binary existence of men and women. Hence the importance, as Judith Butler showed in her book *Gender Trouble*, of the need to problematize the dangers of the identitarian mechanisms particular to feminist struggles that could end up reinforcing the positions assigned by the patriarchy (Butler, 1990). Isn't one of the great contributions of feminism the insistence that the reified distinction between men and women is the result of the totalizing logic of the masculine?

There are, therefore, two positions we could take *toward* the masculine: one that assumes the existence of two completely separate sexes, as if the identity of each sex had its own self-determined existence. Thus, the elimination of one (the male) means the freedom of the other (the female). The other view focuses instead on the problem of love (between female and male) and invites us to interrogate the classic "masculine" dichotomy of the feminine and the masculine. Or, in other words, it helps us understand that it is the masculine locus of enunciation that has tended to create a totalizing and biologistic (positivized) separation between the two sexes (Irigaray, 1985b; Braidotti, 2002). To embrace the logic of the first argument – i.e. that the masculine is by its very nature something to reject and destroy – means nothing other than reproducing what we thought we were fighting.

From the other perspective, the female, the feminine, and the masculine are not previously existing realities – totalities – but two mutually contaminated modes of naming the antagonism that constitutes us as subjects. Or, as Žižek says, it is the recognition that my "identity is thwarted from within by the other" (Žižek, 2013: 771), and that the one – female – and the other – male – are nothing but ways of expressing the inconsistency of the de-totalized reality of masculine closure, which allows us to understand the body in a debiologized way that is configured by the tension between these two loci of enunciation.

If there is something truly revolutionary in the feminine – that socio-historical form expelled from the masculine field – if there is something that capitalism fails to capture from it, it is the detotalization of female desire toward the masculine, but also the detotalization of the place of female desire when it assumes its own right to materialize in public life. From this other side of desire, then, female and male are not understood as a simple "opposition" – typical of masculine discourse – but as selves contaminated from within by the other of the self,[14] whose perseverance continues to work on and shape the feminine and masculine on the basis of difference and processes of identification not idealized by the masculine perspective. Thus, if heteropatriarchal desire represents a totalizing and identitarian retreat from the word, politics, and reason, female desire by contrast brings to light the constitutive difference that organizes them from within.

But we would like to problematize a certain fixation that seems to be present in Copjec's ontology of sexual difference and that could be seen as a sort of inherited patriarchal remnant at the heart of psychoanalytic theory itself. In "Theoretical Problems, Political Problems," Paula Biglieri and Gloria Perelló (2019) wonder what happens to thought when we assume, on the one hand, that patriarchy is one of the oldest forms of socio-historic domination, and, on the other, that "the socio-historical order informs those categories through which we theorize the ontological." This question allows them to formulate the idea that, since theoretical categories are produced in a specific socio-historical context, they cannot escape it. In the authors' words: "these categories are 'contaminated' with ontic content because that is the only way they can they be inscribed within the dominant discourse of the time" (Biglieri and Perelló, 2019). This allows them to go a step further and ask to what extent the ontological categories of psychoanalysis are contaminated by patriarchy? And, therefore, how can we "rethink theoretical formulations in a symbolic universe that incorporates the new modes of social organization resulting from the achievement of equal rights in recent years" (Biglieri and Perelló, 2019)? Here, the feminine point of view, or the feminization of the political, would perform a double operation: from the ontic perspective, it is the materially existing force that allows us to short-circuit from within the master's totalizing discourse embodied in the figure of the dominant, white, heterosexual man. But, from the ontological perspective, it is a catacretic figure used to think when names *fail* (and based on the very acknowledgment of this constitutive *failure*).

Populist feminism (or the antagonism of care)

Now we find ourselves on the other side of the problem that we raised at the beginning of this essay – namely, how to radicalize populism through feminism. Recall that in Essay 2 we rejected the distinction between left-wing populism and right-wing populism, and we offered in turn an interpretation of why we believe that populism is an emancipatory and anti-fascist form of political articulation. What remains for us to explore is whether that form of building the popular, that way of configuring a failed image of the people, is capable of being established through the problems of contemporary feminism. For this, we will think about two current images: the Not One Less movement, and Cristina Fernández de Kirchner's phrase that "The Homeland is the Other."[15]

The signifier Not One Less is an expression that began to take shape in the streets to demand an end to the deaths of women through gendered violence. It was then extended to a rejection of structural adjustment policies and expanded into a global defense of the decriminalization of voluntary abortion. One of its best-known slogans has been: "Contraceptives to not abort. Legal abortion to not die." In principle, we could consider this a specific demand that concerns a particular group – women – such that some theorists of critical and emancipatory thought might consider it secondary to the rest of the demands inscribed within the popular field. But what happens if we begin to think of this demand as one that concerns the very configuration of what we understand to be the popular field, and thereby as having the power to articulate and overdetermine other demands?

The first thing to note is that, out of all the expressions of materially existing struggles in the streets, Not One Less is the one with the greatest ability to cross national borders. While born as a popular movement in Argentina, it quickly spread to different Latin American countries and to other continents of the world, becoming an internationalist signifier with the power to call together different types of massive popular demonstrations. Along with other feminist movements, it even called into question the depoliticized status quo that had for decades celebrated March 8 as "International Women's Day," seemingly reducing it to an empty celebration of women's place in society. Against this depoliticizing process, Not One Less has managed to reconnect with the history of past strikes through which women collectively protested against forms of capitalist oppression and, in turn, exposed their unequal role in society with respect to men. All of which today gives us a massive, global, historical image of living resistance and struggles against patriarchy.

Put in populist terms, the 8M (8 March) strike expresses the ability to organize an antagonistic image or configuration of society divided between those who seek to maintain this form of oppression and those of us who seek to destroy it. But, still more, it allows us to understand that femicides, austerity policies against women, and the rejection of legal abortion are not simply capricious attacks against a particular group, but represent the very limit of patriarchy as a dominant social relationship: the social reproduction of life. It is, in short, a specific kind of social relationship in which those called women and those called men occupy an unequal position. And that inequality is reiterated in the popular field and in its organization forms when it comes to fighting for terrain against those on top, such that unions and plebeian social and political movements have been predominantly male spaces, despite the fact that forms of exploitation have been shared by this "strategic" gender division. This does not mean simply discarding those historic forms of struggle led by men, but admitting that "gender" inequality has permeated the structure of the popular field itself. And, above all, it means also admitting that it was from within this same field that the current socio-historic power of feminism became imaginable. So, the interpellative power that feminism enjoys right now already represents a restructuring of the symbolic register of the popular field, and therefore a reconfiguration of how the antagonistic division of the social between the elites and the people is produced. And this is despite the failed strategies by some elites to appropriate feminist discourse and reduce it to competition for jobs and the redistribution of power in the labor market.

Feminist populism (or the homeland is the other)

Now that it is clear that feminist struggles should be considered a matter of first-order importance within the construction of the popular camp, let's explore a bit more the link between populism and care. To do so, we are going to begin with that bond of love that we mentioned in the previous section in relation to Antigone, and that we would now like to return to through the signifier "The Homeland is the Other." In our understanding, this signifier functions as the external limit of fascism. We know it is very difficult to think about the term "love" today, since, while this is a word that never ceases to circulate, it is also true that it has lost its collective character, retreating into the private and individual sphere. But we must not forget how important this term became in the face of the tragic modern experience of lost totality. If we retrospectively read the use thinkers like Hegel have made of this word, we find that love is a way of confronting what one opposes, since the other, far from something to be eliminated, is conceived through the interplay of self-preservation and self-cancellation, i.e. knowing oneself in the other. Doesn't the emancipatory drive of populism reactivate this old problem of love and return it to the collective sphere?

Let's delve a little deeper into the articulatory logic of populism through the question of love. This means starting not from the idea of a previously given identity, but from the possibility of building a collective we (self) through the other of the self. In fascism, the "self" can only exist, on the one hand, through its negation and rejection of the other and, on the other hand, as something previously given. Therefore, fascism is a work of the self where what is opposed is the other to be destroyed, because this is the only way to achieve the completeness of being. From this perspective, working through opposition means dominating and destroying that which has been conceived as "the other." The relationship to the self is therefore understood as a relation of property, as the possession of oneself, of things, and of others. My identity is constituted through an idea of domination. I exist insofar as I dominate, and the other threatens to dominate me. The emancipatory structure of populism's logic of articulation, on the other hand, proposes a different self-relation, a different labor of the self, a different way of working through opposition. We would even dare to say that it is affirmed through a care for the self as the other of the self.

We believe that we can find the key to this idea of care as the other of the self in Cristina Fernández de Kirchner's phrase, "The Homeland is the Other." This phrase allows us to see that the other is the irreducible element that constitutes our self without suppressing it, and so we need to take care of that irreducible element that constitutes us. The other crafts (but does not fix) our identity, configures a we affirmed as the future, as what is to come through equality. In other words, it is a double operation of tolerating differences and building a shared equality. Opposition is therefore not against the other, but against that form of identity that seeks to destroy the irreducible (or heterogeneous) through the configuration of inequality and exclusion. It is not about destroying the other but about destroying a position that prevents the existence of the other (the heterogeneous), what is to come. It antagonizes that power that seeks to assert itself as domination of the self. Emancipatory populism opposes and seeks to destroy the position that tries to eliminate what – from the totalizing point of view – is considered other, i.e. peasants, indigenous people, women, LGBTI+ people, etc.

And this is how we find the fundamental difference between the notion of care proposed through an autonomist matrix and the notion of care explored through a populist matrix. If the first sets out from an affirmative power (*potencia*) that does not need to produce articulations for the construction of the political – since its *potencia* gives itself form through its constitutive immanence and its confidence in affirmative completeness – the second, on the other hand, assumes that care is a constant labor of opposition (negativity); and that the challenge is not so much to renounce working with negativity (as affirmative ontology seems to do) as it is to work through this opposition (negativity) differently. That is, to develop a form of work that is not articulated through domination of the other but instead embraces the other of the self as that *polemos* that must be cared for in order for things to flourish.

It is possible that this type of political articulation, these new images encouraged by a populist feminism, are the best way to destroy patriarchy and the form of property and domination associated with it, and the beginning of a new kind of social relationship that transforms the conception of property as domination. This is a labor of the self that begins to move away from the extractive logic of surplus value and exploitation. This is why, faced with patriarchal domination, populist feminism could give shape evidentially to a form of common usage for those of us who believe that we have nothing in common, those who embrace the constitutive irreducibility of every singularity as the secret that allows us to imagine an egalitarian and republican life with others. This is probably a form of feminism that is yet to be explored within a populism that perseveres and that, like an irreducible secret, cannot be sacrificed.

Notes

Foreword

1 www.journalofdemocracy.org/articles/the-populist-challenge-to-liberal-democracy.

2 "How Does Populism Turn Authoritarian? Venezuela Is a Case in Point": www.nytimes.com/2017/04/01/world/americas/venezuela-populism-authoritarianism.html, www.theatlantic.com/international/archive/2017/06/venezuela-populism-fail/525321.

3 See Stephan Hahn, summarizing William Galston's view, in "The Populist Specter," *The Nation*, January 28 – February 4, 2019: www.thenation.com/article/archive/mounk-galston-deneen-eichengreen-the-populist-specter.

4 "Militant" is an important part of Biglieri and Cadahia's political theoretical vocabulary. The term translates awkwardly into English, especially American English, where it signifies dogmatic and aggressive and hardened political views and a tendency toward extreme, sometimes violent, actions. By contrast, in French, Spanish, and Italian, its meaning is closer to political engagement as part of a cause, or what Biglieri and Cadahia call collective belonging. In fact, they insist, an emancipatory populist militant has precisely to be non-dogmatic. It would be, they wrote in an email to me, "someone who escapes dogmatism, someone who defends some principles and belongs to a collective formation or organization but, at the same time, is never fully captured by

those principles, collective formation and organization. That is to say, someone who is always open to the new, to the critique, to the event."

5 Occupy, it is important to remember, began as a protest against *Citizens United,* the 2011 Supreme Court decision delivering the *coup de grâce* to electoral democracy by lifting restrictions on corporate financing of campaigns.

Introduction

1 These soft coups began in 2009 with the removal of Manuel Zelaya in Honduras, followed by coups against Fernando Lugo in Paraguay in 2012, Dilma Rousseff in 2016, and Evo Morales in 2019. And we consider these to be "paradoxically" democratic coups for two reasons. In the first place, because they do not break with the institutional order in the old style of the civilian–military coups of the second half of the twentieth century in Latin America, which explicitly suspended the rule of law and functioned through a permanent state of exception with an alternative juridical order. And, in the second place, because juridical–mediatic complicity creates the fiction of a procedure regulated within the rules of the institutional game.

2 For the Latin American right, it has become common practice to persecute judicially popular political leaders once their mandates have ended. This persecution has been called "lawfare" and consists of establishing a link of complicity between some sectors of the judicial branch, corporate–media power, and right-wing presidents. This complicity consists of creating mediatic–judicial cases without any proof or constitutional guarantees whatsoever, through which misleading corruption charges are filed. These cases are managed and tried by judges allied with the mediatic–judicial apparatus, with the goal of damaging the leader's image nationally and internationally and preventing their return to electoral politics.

3 Recall that, in Colombia, during the second term of Juan Manuel Santos, a peace agreement was signed between one of Latin America's oldest guerrilla organizations (the FARC) and the Colombian government. This peace agreement meant the end of the armed struggle, the disarming of guerrillas, their transition into a political party, and a pact to carry out a series of key reforms for the country. However, after the victory of far-right leader Iván Duque in the most recent elections, the peace process suffered a setback at the hands of the current

government, which has translated into the suspension of the process and the return of the logic of war.

4 Biglieri and Perelló (2007).
5 Coronel and Cadahia (2018).
6 Cadahia, Coronel, Valeria, and Ramírez (2018).
7 This project was financed by the British Academy, led by Mark Devenney and Paula Biglieri, and carried out by the Centre for Applied Philosophy, Politics, and Ethics at the University of Brighton, and the Ernesto Laclau Open Seminar at the Faculty of Philosophy and Letters of the University of Buenos Aires.
8 The Consortium is co-directed by Professor Judith Butler (University of California–Berkeley) and Professor Penelope Deutscher (Northwestern University). See https://criticaltheory-consortium.org.

Essay 1 The Secret of Populism

1 At the beginning of the 1990s, after the fall of the Berlin Wall, the English economist John Williamson drafted the first formulation of the "Washington Consensus," which initially took the form of a series of neoliberal recommendations but soon became a menu of demands required of developing countries. This "consensus" would come to be the guiding axis for policies imparted by the political-economic-intellectual complex comprising the US Federal Administration and Treasury and international financial organs (the International Monetary Fund, World Bank, Inter-American Development Bank, etc.).
2 The various forms of modernization theory and comparative politics and culture (informed by authors such as Gabriel Almond and followers like Seymour M. Lipset, etc.) argued that: "The transition from one society to another is moreover inscribed on a continuum that does not allow for profound ruptures. To the contrary, this evolution emerges gradually and progressively and entails the existence of improvement and progress (in positivist terms) between both extremes of said continuum" (Zapata, 1990: 172).
3 Badie and Hermet refer to the three traditional Latin American cases of Juan D. Perón in Argentina, Getulio Vargas in Brazil, and Lázaro Cárdenas in Mexico, to which they add the examples of Kemal Ataturk in Turkey, Nasser in Egypt, Bourguiba in Tunisia, and Ferdinand Marcos in the Philippines.
4 In Essay 4, we will return in more detail to the relationship between populism and republicanism.

5 The category of *Bonapartism* (which is interchangeable with *Caesarism*) has a long pedigree in Marxist research. In general terms, it was used to work through the autonomy or heteronomy of politics vis-à-vis the economic dimension. For example, Karl Marx himself used it in the *Eighteenth Brumaire of Louis Bonaparte* (1869) to analyze the dictatorship of Louis Napoléon, and Friedrich Engels made use of it to address the Bismarck period in *The Role of Force in History* (1887).

6 We will develop this idea later.

7 According to Laclau and Mouffe (1985), a hegemonic articulation presupposes the operation of two opposing logics on the same terrain: the logic of equivalence and the logic of difference. Chains of equivalence do not come together because their particularities have a shared objective, since the implicated elements are defined negatively, as differences. Their particular interests are extremely diverse, but their demands are nevertheless equivalent vis-à-vis an excluded element. That is to say, the logic of equivalence interrupts the logic of difference insofar as the elements are equivalent to one another with respect to what is excluded. This chain of equivalences unifies around a signifier or element that represents them, which is nothing other than one of these particularities that has assumed representation of the totality, insofar as it becomes emptied of its particular characteristics. This hegemonizing particularity functions as an empty signifier – and, the emptier it is, the more elements can enter into equivalency in the chain vis-à-vis the excluded element.

Essay 2 Neither Left nor Right: Populism without Apology

1 This particular element – which turns out to be an empty signifier – assumes such representation because it is overdetermined and condenses the greatest number of associative chains in a given social order. This is why representation in a hegemonic articulation is constitutively distorted and takes place amid a tense negotiation between the particular and the universal.

2 This paper was presented at the conference "Fascism? Populism? Democracy?" organized by the International Consortium of Critical Theory Programs at the University of Brighton, and has not yet been published, so we are only able to cite the transcript.

3 In the Introduction, note 2, we described the functioning of this

practice of judicial – and therefore political – persecution that has been called "lawfare."

4 Mauricio Macri governed Argentina between 2015 and 2019 thanks to an alliance among different right-wing sectors. In 2019, and with the backing of this same alliance, he failed in his reelection attempt and was defeated in the first round by the populist ticket made up of Alberto Fernández and Cristina Fernández de Kirchner.

5 See www.lanacion.com.ar/1903034-gonzalez-fraga-le-hicieron-creer-al-empleado-medio-que-podia-comprarse-plasmas-y-viajar-al-exterior, consulted 21/05/2019.

6 See www.ambito.com/841192-les-hicieron-creer-que-podian-vivir-de-esa-forma-eternamente.

7 Lacan introduces the notion of capitalist discourse in his 1953 "Rome Speech" ("The Function and Field of Speech and Language in Psychoanalysis").

8 Laclau writes: "Dislocation is the source of freedom. But this is not the freedom of a subject with a *positive* identity – in which case it would just be a structural locus; rather it is merely the freedom of a structural fault which can only construct an identity through acts of *identification*" (1990: 60).

9 We will address this link between fascism and neoliberalism in greater detail in the next essay.

Essay 3 Against Neoliberal Fascism: From Sacrificial Identity to Egalitarian Singularity

1 We refer here to the notion of constitutive lack of both the social being and the subject, which we discussed in detail through Laclau and Alemán in the previous essay.

2 In the first essay, we put forward a critique of this text.

3 The Audiovisual Communication Services Law (known as the Media Law) was enacted in 2011 during the government of Cristina Fernández de Kirchner and entailed the attempt to standardize the functioning and distribution of audio-visual media licenses in Argentina. This meant repealing the old existing law from the last civilian–military dictatorship, which encouraged the accumulation of licenses in the hands of small groups and distorted the social meaning of communication in terms of rights. The Equal Marriage Law was also enacted during the Fernández de Kirchner government in 2010, making Argentina the first Latin American country to recognize same-sex marriage. The nationalization of water in Bolivia was

one of the rallying cries of the constituent process that Evo Morales sponsored after winning his first election, and meant putting an end to water privatization strategies in Bolivia. Along these lines, the new Political Constitution of the Plurinational State, approved by referendum in January 2009, incorporated a new conception of water, understood as a common good and a fundamental human right. Beginning in 2008, the government of Rafael Correa supported labor regulation for domestic workers in Ecuador in light of the precarity, informality, and exploitation they experienced. One of the most important measures consisted of requiring employers to register their workers for social security.

4 While in Essays 1 and 2 we developed our understanding of the ontological dimension of populism, it's worth mentioning that what interests us here is to underline two things: its indeterminacy and its equivalential function.

5 We will return in more detail to this question in the last section of this essay.

6 In the next essay, we will analyze in more detail the question of populism and its link to republicanism. In this section, we are only interested in laying out the arguments according to which some republican authors formulate a proximity between populism and republicanism.

7 We refer to the limits of populism for interpellating the middle classes and shaping a political subject beyond the demand for consumer goods.

Essay 4 Profaning the Public: The Plebeian Dimension of Republican Populism

1 In Essay 5, we will return to the debate on the role of the leader from a psychoanalytic perspective.

2 Institutional logic appears in Laclau's work through what he calls the logic of difference, which always functions inseparably from the logic of equivalence. Likewise, we can find it in the very constitution of the populist people insofar as it is traversed by organizations. But we will address this last aspect in the next essay (see also Essay 1).

3 We will return to a discussion of the decision, but from a psychoanalytic angle, in Essay 6.

4 Among the most emblematic cases, we could emphasize the murders of Berta Cáceres and Lesbia Yaneth Urquía in Honduras, and Marielle Franco in Brazil, or the exponential

growth of such killings in places like Colombia where, in a single year (2018), 266 social movement and territorial leaders were assassinated.

5 By "para-state alliances," we refer to links between state powers and organized crime (paramilitaries, drug cartels, etc.).

6 We are grateful for this citation to the Cuban historian and theorist Julio Guanche, who is also carrying out detailed research on republicanism and populism in 1930s Cuba.

Essay 5   Toward an Internationalist Populism

1 It's worth mentioning that, as we write this book, Berta Cáceres and Marielle Franco have been assassinated, Rafael Correa is in exile in Brussels, Cristina Fernández de Kirchner and Gustavo Petro are experiencing all kinds of mediatic and judicial persecution in their countries, and Francia Márquez has suffered an attempt on her life that nearly killed her.

2 See Augusto Monterroso's (2013) critique of Mario Vargas Llosa, who personally took on the task of editing a collective volume on the danger of authoritarian leadership in Latin America. Although the book project was cut short, Vargas Llosa was one of the main Latin American intellectuals to dissassociate the figure of the authoritarian leader from Europe and identify it with Latin America.

3 We will return to this point in Essay 6.

4 On this point, we follow the detailed analysis of Laclau's use of Freud's texts in Biglieri and Perelló (2012).

5 Freud announces the idea of destabilizing the normal/pathological binary in the very title of his text *The Psychopathology of Everyday Life* (1989b [1901]).

6 Freud mentions three different types of identification: the first with the father, the second with the love-object, and the third that we find in the mutual link between members of the group.

7 When Freud makes this argument, he is responding to those who argue that, by joining the group, subjects lose the characteristics of an individual (rationality, etc.).

8 "It is the articulations of demands that make the difference. Demands stage what is not considered in the Freudian schema (or at least what was not systematically considered by Freud) – need and desire. From a Lacanian perspective these two orders configure the notion of demand" (Biglieri and Perelló, 2016: 24).

9 See www.youtube.com/watch?v=DmIwRGInWDc.

10 Gramsci was read and translated in Argentina, beginning in 1947.

11 It's worth pointing out that, in the 1920s, José Carlos Mariátegui traveled to Italy and would be very influenced by intellectual debates there, reading several important authors of the moment, such as Piero Gobetti, Benedetto Croce, and Georges Sorel. They would all help him think through the problem of aesthetics within revolutionary processes, and would also help him to arrive at similar theses to those developed by Antonio Gramsci in *Prison Notebooks* on the problem of the national-popular and the possibilities for Marxisms in peripheral countries. While Mariátegui didn't have the opportunity to discover these similarities between his thought and Gramsci's, since the *Notebooks* were only published after his death, there are indications that Mariátegui was indeed aware of Gramsci's journalistic work, since, as an assiduous reader of the journal founded by Gramsci and Terracini, *L'Ordine Nuovo*, he would come to say, in a note written for the newspaper *El Tiempo*, that the journal's founders were "two of the party's most notable intellectuals: Terracini and Gramsci" (Mariátegui, 1921).

12 One thing that we should keep in mind has to do with the difficulties populist thought has in addressing aesthetic problems.

13 In Mariátegui's case, this is found in "Literature on Trial," the last of his *Seven Interpretive Essays on Peruvian Reality* (1971), and, in Gramsci's case, in a compendium of texts included in the *Prison Notebooks*, which would be given the name "Literature and National Life" (1998).

14 The concept of "situated universalism" is being developed by the Colombian anthropologist José Figueroa within the framework of the project "Situated Universalism: Radical Liberalism, Afro-Descendency, and Nation in Cuba and Ecuador." While these works have not yet been published, we have had access to them through conversations and unpublished manuscripts. For more information on his work, see: www.calas.lat/es/content/jose-antonio-figueroa.

15 We could also include here the research project "Theorising Transnational Politics," financed by the British Academy and carried out by the Centre for Applied Philosophy, Politics, and Ethics (CAPPE) at the University of Brighton and the Ernesto Laclau Open Seminar in the Faculty of Philosophy and Letters of the University of Buenos Aires, between 2015 and 2018.

16 Recall that the "Troika" is the popular (and pejorative) name for the trident of supranational institutions made up of the

European Commission, the European Central Bank, and the International Monetary Fund.

17 We refer to the MeRA25, the Greek European Realistic Disobedience Front, and Germany's Demokratie in Europa. In fact, in the July 2019 election in which SYRIZA was defeated, several MeRA25 deputies entered the Greek national parliament, among them Yanis Varoufakis.

18 See the interview with Žižek in *Diario Perfil* (2018).

19 The last civilian–military dictatorship in Argentina was in power from 1976 to 1983, leaving 30,000 disappeared.

20 UNASUR's importance as an alternative international space in the region led it to be one of the first targets attacked and dismantled by the neoliberal governments of Mauricio Macri in Argentina, Jair Bolsonaro in Brazil, and Lenin Moreno in Ecuador. Bear in mind that UNASUR was constituted by 12 nations (Argentina, Bolivia, Brazil, Chile, Colombia, Ecuador, Guyana, Paraguay, Peru, Suriname, Uruguay, and Venezuela). It declared as its formal aim: "the constitution of a space for cultural, economic, and socio-political integration with respect for the particularities of every nation," and it claimed as its main challenge "to eradicate socio-economic inequality, to achieve social inclusion and citizen participation, to strengthen democracy, and to reduce imbalances while respecting the sovereignty and independence of every state." UNASUR turned out to be an active and successful space for the egalitarian participation of the different countries involved. The decision to build political spaces that excluded the United States, and its unconditional ally Canada, weakened the position of the US in the region and allowed for the emergence of a dynamic among member countries guided by notions of horizontality, independence, sovereignty, and the equality of peoples. To give an example: UNASUR played a central role in stopping the 2008 civilian coup d'état threatening Evo Morales in Bolivia. The urgent meeting of UNASUR presidents gathered in Santiago de Chile to strongly back Morales stated in the Declaration of La Moneda that: "They emphatically reject and will not recognize any situation that would entail an attempted civilian coup, an interruption of the institutional order, or any situation that would compromise the territorial integrity of Bolivia" (*Página 12*, 17/09/2008, www.pagina12. com.ar/diario/elmundo/subnotas/111740-35328-2008-09-17. html). UNASUR's intervention isolated the insurrection against the central government by right-wing governors of Bolivia's Media Luna (or Half Moon), the richest part of the country,

leaving them without any support in the region. Moreover, this first effective political action positioned UNASUR as the main political organization in the region, in which political issues could be resolved without the intervention of the US. It is worth noting that, with regard to Bolivia, the US openly harassed the populist government of the moment – for example, endorsing the insurrection by right-wing governors, and including the country on the "blacklist" of countries that weren't doing enough to fight drug trafficking.

Essay 6 The Absent Cause of Populist Militancy

1 We refer here to the concept elaborated by Oliver Marchart in his book *Post-Foundational Political Thought: Political Difference in Nancy, Lefort, Badiou and Laclau* (2007), and the precise use of the term will be explained later.
2 We are alluding here to Jorge Alemán's *Capitalism: The Perfect Crime or Emancipation* (2019), where he utilizes the metaphor of the "perfect crime" to present his hypothesis that neoliberalism is the first historical regime that seeks to capture the subject in its structural dimension. We developed this hypothesis in Essay 2.
3 We elaborated the development of this concept in Essay 3, following Foucault and Brown.
4 We will explain what we mean by "classic schemas of the left" in what follows.
5 Jorge Abelardo Ramos (Buenos Aires, 1921–94) was a politician, intellectual, and journalist, and a founder of the National Left, the political current that Laclau was a member of during his youth in Argentina. Among Ramos' most oustanding works was *Revolution and Counter-Revolution in Argentina* (2006 [1957]) – originally published in 1957 and then republished and reformulated on several occasions – and *History of the Latin American Nation* (2011 [1968]) in 1968.
6 See   www.pagina12.com.ar/diario/elpais/1-85297-2007-05-21. html.
7 Through *New Reflections on the Revolution of Our Time* (Laclau, 1990), we can equate the notions of necessity and sedimentation and argue that the latter is nothing more than an always partial and failed attempt to limit reactivation.
8 This distinction sets out from the idea of accidentality – derived

from Aristotle's *Metaphysics* – which refers to those characteristics of an object that do not relate to its essence.

9 Lacan discusses the *tuché* and *automaton* in his 1964 *Seminar*
(1998 [1964]).

10 "Cycle of rebellion" refers to the period characterized by an
expansion of social demands and antagonisms that various
neoliberal governments were incapable of domesticating.
Marked by a constant repression of indigenous coca farmers
and any kind of social protest, the cycle of rebellion gave rise
to what Álvaro García Linera (2008) – Vice-President of the
Plurinational State of Bolivia from 2006 to 2019 – defined as a
popular indigenous articulation. The coca farmers – who resisted
attempts to eradicate the coca leaf and relocate their communities – established an equivalential chain with a diversity of
demands tied to the "defense of natural resources." In fact, these
demands were presented as a matter of "national sovereignty."
Thus, defending the coca leaf meant defending ancestral traditions; defending water against privatization and rate increases
in Cochabamba meant defending national health (in what was
known as the "water war"); the massive blockade of La Paz led
by Felipe Quispe – who would later become an opponent of Evo
Morales – demanding free access to land, water, and the coca
leaf, and opposing the export of gas to the US for a pittance
(the "gas war") meant defending natural resources against
foreign plunder; and the demand for a constituent assembly
meant fighting for a new constitution that would protect natural
resources and recognize indigenous peoples, etc.

11 The 15-M, or Indignados Movement, began with the irruption
of protest on May 15, 2011, in Madrid, but quickly spread
across Spain. It began when a group of protesters decided to
camp out in the Puerta del Sol, quickly becoming massive.
While the demands were diverse, they centered on the idea
that "they do not represent us" and expressed a generalized
rejection of the political establishment – consisting basically of
the Popular Party (PP) and the Spanish Socialist Workers' Party
(PSOE) – and the financial establishment, i.e. the banks.

12 The MAS (Movement for Socialism) is the political party of the
coca farmers' unions.

13 Here it is interesting to specify that "dislocation is the very
form of temporality. And temporality must be conceived as the
exact opposite of space. The 'spatialization' of an event consists
of eliminating its temporality" (Laclau, 1990: 41). That is to
say, while the effort to endure brings the deadening effect of a
routine that seeks to reduce all variation to an invariant nucleus

(space is the field of structural repetition), time, on the contrary, is an event that is irreducible to those elements pre-established by the structure.

14 The "circles" were the organizational form that Podemos gave rise to, and were groups governed basically by horizontality and participation, in which different people converge according to their interests. There were two types of circles: territorially anchored circles, and thematic circles based on programmatic field or professional interest. These circles enjoyed autonomy as long as they respected the general principles sketched out by the Citizens' Assembly. Moreover, any person – even without being a member of Podemos – was authorized to start a circle and gain "active" status to achieve official recognition.

15 In Essays 2 and 3, we commented on a whole series of these kinds of critiques.

16 We owe this reading of Bataille to Oliver Marchart (2006).

17 Lacan discusses the notion of the absent cause in the 1964 text "Presence of the Analyst" (1998 [1964]: 123–35).

Essay 7 We Populists are Feminists

1 There exists a fruitful debate between theorists of sexual difference (Irigaray, Cixous, Clément), anti-sexual difference (Plaza, Wittig, and Delphy), queer and gender theorists (cf. Braidotti and Butler, 1994: 27–61; Butler, 1990), and Lacanian feminists (Copjec, 2002), about whether it is or is not possible to use expressions like "feminine" or "woman." With regard to the first current, authors like Luce Irigaray (1993, 1985b) and Rosi Braidotti (2004, 2002) embrace the need to inhabit these terms as a paradox, and to grant them a non-essentialist usage not determined a priori. That is to say, they see the need to consider these words as the name given to a form of exclusion, and thus to determine whether, through this exclusion, a "female feminism" is feasible as a political, historical, contingent, and non-essentialist project open to the multiplicity of forms for being and existing in society (Braidotti, 1991). With regard to the second current, thinkers like Monique Plaza and Monique Wittig believe that these categories associated with sexual difference become too essentialist, since they lend themselves to an ahistoric or apolitical interpretation of problems, and reintroduce the symmetrical binary of male/female (Braidotti and Butler, 1994: 48). The third current, echoing the second, also believes that these terms

retain a metaphysical aftertaste traversed by an essentialist "heterosexual matrix" from which authors like Judith Butler and Paul Preciado seek to distance themselves (Butler, 1990: 35; Preciado, 2002).

Within these three currents (sexual difference, anti-sexual difference, and queer and gender theory), the question emerges in two fundamental, but not unique, ways. The first question asks whether the use of expressions like "feminine" or "woman" implies the reactivation of an essentialism. The second, by contrast, is a question about the problem of desire, whose tension fluctuates according to whether we are dealing with a heterosexual tradition (sexual difference), lesbian tradition (gender theory), or whether these are two different traditions for naming female homosexuality (Braidotti and Butler, 1994: 47–8). If it is the first, then, lesbian desire would be independent of female desire and the category of woman should be dissolved. But if it is the second, then lesbian desire functions on a continuum of female sexuality. With regard to Lacanian feminists, we could say that they distance themselves from all of the currents mentioned above in two fundamental aspects: the negative character of desire, and the place assigned to the feminine in Lacan's theory.

Now, it seems to us that terms like "feminine" or "woman" are completely obsolete if we understand them as a mere datum, a biological fact, or an ahistorical metaphysical essence that would establish in an essentialist way a society divided between "men" and "women" – with an entire series of historical associations assigned to each gender. However, if we think about "the feminine" and "the woman" from within the debates that we just mentioned, we find contradictory positions and the debate is far from over. Even more so, this debate is not resolved if we take into consideration the uses assigned to these words by feminist authors of sexual difference, Lacanian feminism, or even the use given in the contemporary political experiences of Latin American feminism in which our own militancy is inscribed. In this sense, it seems interesting to follow some reflections by Braidotti and Joan Scott (although we do not share their Derridean and Deleuzian ontological assumptions about affirmative difference), who believe that "it is not by willful self-naming that we shall find the exit from the prison-house of phallogocentric language" (Braidotti and Butler, 1994: 51). That's why renouncing the use of expressions like "woman" and "feminine" – and looking for other categories to theorize these problems – does not entail an automatic transformation of the material structures of power with which those old names were associated (Scott, 1986).

Moreover, we would add, sophisticated debates often occur within academia that wind up distancing themselves from the sphere of concrete political struggles, and the terms that these same struggles use to express their discontent and to seek social transformation. We share with Braidotti the idea that this attitude of renouncing certain words can lead to a kind of naïve voluntarism of naming – as if, by naming things differently, we were already creating the new and pushing back oppressive logics – that, paradoxically, reactivates the worst remnants of the omnipotence of theories of consciousness. As if the choice to name ourselves differently would free us automatically from the socio-historic ties that escape to the level of consciousness, and we would be able to control – through the mere act of naming – the being of our subjectivity. This doesn't mean that there isn't a defiance in beginning to name things differently and expressing the experimental and performative on the order of being, but this experimental game doesn't need to come at the expense of those who continue to use terms like "woman" or "female," and nor does it imply that these expressions retain a patriarchal metaphysics. Perhaps the problem lies in believing that the name exhausts our entire identity, and that once we name things differently it is possible to recuperate the purity of one's being. Perhaps the secret of emancipation is not so much about assigning the "correct name" as it is about theoretical movements that support our contaminated and non-totalizing use of words to name the world.

We prefer to play with expressions in an attempt to distrust these very words, to the point of encouraging dirty contaminations. So "changes in the deep structures of identity require socio-symbolic interventions that go beyond willful self-naming," i.e. assuming that "unconscious processes are trans-historical and consequently require *time* to be changed was not supposed to mean that we can step outside or beside the unconscious by making a counter-move towards 'historical or social reality.' It rather means that to make effective political choices we must come to terms with the specific temporality of the unconscious" (Braidotti and Butler, 1994: 51). This is why, Braidotti adds, it can be interesting to embrace the paradox of feminine identity as something that "needs to be both claimed and deconstructed" (51), with the objective of understanding the "feminine" and the "woman" as a situated knowledge or a "politics of location." And undoing the essentialist and oppressive dimensions of these terms can come at the same time through claiming them affirmatively as a project within a force field, i.e. as a symbolic and political "position" (42). On the one hand, this is because using expressions like "woman" and "feminine" does not need to mean that all women are the same or that we are referring mechanically to a naturalized identity. And, on the other hand, because it can serve as a platform for political action by and for women, no longer understood as the name of a previously given identity but as a relational position to be built collectively. In other words, it is a subject-position, in the political and militant sense, that takes on both historic sedimentation and, at the same time, the contingency and indeterminacy characteristic of all transformative practice.

2 We choose the figures of the feminine and the popular because we are interested in emphasizing several questions. In the first place, and following Braidotti, these can function as "conceptual *personae*" in a scene, which – without denying the existence of other personae – "illuminate ... aspects of one's practice which were blind spots before" and that are "materially embedded" in the subject (Braidotti, 2002: 13). In the second place, we choose them because these figures express a constitutive paradox whose contradictory character does not seek to be "overcome" but simply worked through differently. In other words, the feminine and the popular express both a locus of (historically sedimented) oppression and a political position (an emancipatory possibility). And in the third place, these figures, by having the peculiarity of setting into motion both intelligence and feeling, are capable of affecting us in such a way as to mobilize us for political action.

3 It should be noted that feminism in Latin America has its own evolution, so much so that it is characterized by four moments or waves whose genealogies do not coincide with either European or North American feminism (Rivera Berruz, 2018). The colonial experience and the condition of periphery within the geopolitical scenario has marked a singular drift in both feminist thought and praxis in Latin America. In this regard, the 1980s and 1990s marked a turning point in the feminist field that eventually divided itself between institutionalist feminists, militant feminists, and autonomous feminists. The first trend was associated with the figure of professional feminists linked to institutional work within international organizations and NGOs in the period of the neoliberal states. The other two trends, on the other hand, were more associated with grassroots work with social movements. However, while militant feminists

did not renounce their left-wing political parties or unions, the autonomous feminists, on the other hand, considered it a priority to create an autonomous women's movement regardless of political orientation or affiliation (Gargallo, 2006). Parallel to this was the need to demonstrate the specificity of black feminism (Carneiro, 2000; Gonzalez, 2015; Curiel, 2016, 2007), lesbian feminism (Espinosa Miñoso, 2011), and indigenous feminism (Bastian Duarte, 2012; Rivera Berruz, 2018; Rivera Cusicanqui, 2018), whose forms of emancipation had to deal with a number of issues that classical feminism had not yet raised. Currently, there seems to be a new reorganization of the feminist field that involves two highly relevant issues. On the one hand is the need to articulate the plurality of Latin American feminisms (autonomist, militant, black, indigenous, lesbian, queer) with other struggles of the popular field (class and race), and, on the other, the need to rethink what type of link has been brewing between the state and feminism, outside the consensual logic of the neoliberal model. This is where we place our bet– namely, on the question of how to think about a feminism within the popular field, and its capacity to shape a popular and feminist state. This approach would resonate with the work of feminists such as Sueli Carneiro (2000), María Luisa Femenías (2007), Sonia Álvarez (1998), Alba Carosio (2009), and Marlise Matos and Clarisse Paradise (2013), among others.

4 Braidotti expresses this critique of negativity by feminists of difference very well when she rejects the role that the concept plays for Butler and Žižek. According to the author, the role of negativity leads to a sort of melancholy that would become incapable of advocating for social transformation (Braidotti, 2002: 52–64). We reject this equation of negativity with stagnant melancholy. We don't believe that this is to be found in Butler's ethical proposal, and that, like Butler, authors like Laclau help us to theorize emancipation precisely through the constitutive negativity or gap of the subject (or social being).

5 We believe that this rejection of antagonism and negativity is deeply rooted in both European difference feminism and Latin American autonomist feminism. As to the first, we refer to feminist proposals anchored in the theory of difference, *l'écriture féminine*, and some renewals of queer and gender theory that embrace ontological difference in its constitutively affirmative dimension, without passing through the play of negativity. The most important representatives of this approach include authors like Luce Irigaray, Rosi Braidotti, and Paul Preciado, who pick up from Deleuzian and/or Derridean approaches to thinking

difference from within the self and beyond the negativity of either the dialectic of difference and identity, or aspects of the Lacanian legacy (Irigaray, 1985b; Braidotti, 2004, 2002; Preciado, 2016).

By "autonomist feminism," we refer to those post-Marxist feminist approaches that take from authors like Hardt, Negri, and Deleuze a contemporary re-reading of power (*potencia*), desire, and the common in Spinoza, in order to theorize emancipation, and also those authors who work on the question of communitarian feminism as an alternative to the colonial legacy from the perspective of decolonial theory. With regard to the post-Marxist current, we find authors like Verónica Gago (2017, 2020), who takes up ideas of power (*potencia*), desire, and life in common from the perspective of an affirmative ontology that rejects any vestige of theoretical negativity [in Spanish, and in autonomist literature in particular, we find a bifurcation between *poder* as "power-over" and *potencia* as a more essentially positive "power-to" – Trans.].

With regard to postcolonial feminism, we find the work of María Lugones (2011), Rita Segato (2013), Silvia Rivera Cusicanqui (2018), Raquel Gutiérrez Aguilar (2017), and María Galindo (2004). Both post-Marxist and communitarian feminisms tend to establish a whole series of oppositions that would seem to define the privileged locations for emancipation ahead of time. Thus the state, representation, political parties, the figure of the leader, and confrontation tend to fall on the side of abstraction and patriarchy, while life in common, immanence, new forms of feminist organizing, and the body fall on the side of emancipatory feminism. It is possible that this convergence between European difference feminism and Latin American autonomist feminism results from their affirmative conception of desire, which moves away from the view of desire as negativity typical of the Hegelian, Lacanian, and even the populist traditions.

6 Here Gago reiterates a whole series of prejudices typical of Latin American autonomism, which we analyzed in Essay 3.

7 By the feminization of the popular, we refer to three things: in the first place, the need for leadership figures put forth by women; in the second place, the need to build imaginaries and rituals on the basis of the desires of those who have historically occupied the "position" of women; and, in the third place, the role that women have played in staging the capitalist contradiction of social reproduction that is historically associated with care work (Fraser, 2016).

8 While an extensive bibliography exists on the problem of care and the various approaches to it (Vega Solís, 2009, 2015), what interests us here is to focus on the idea of the crisis of care proposed by Nancy Fraser in her article "Contradictions of Capitalism and Care" (2016). Along these lines, we take up the distinction between social reproduction (care work) and the social production of value (labor) as two ways of experiencing the social contradiction of capital within capitalism's financialized phase. In the historical distribution of gender roles, the former has been associated with women, and the latter with men. According to Fraser, in the current phase of financialized capitalism, we are witnessing a "crisis of care" because this dimension of reproduction seeks to be invisibilized as a first-order political problem (women have entered the labor market, the state does not offer social protection, and care work is relegated to a precarious and informal labor market among popular sectors).

9 It is worth noting that this view of knowledge has many resonances with Adrienne Rich's (1994) proposal in the 1980s for a "politics of location," which was later taken up by Braidotti. For Braidotti, "The politics of location means that the thinking, the theoretical process, is not abstract, universalized, objective, and detached, but rather that it is situated in the contingency of one's experience and as such it is a necessarily *partial* exercise. In other words, one's intellectual vision is not a disembodied mental activity; rather, it is closely connected to one's place of enunciation, i.e., where one is actually speaking from" (Braidotti, 1991: 160).

10 We refer to the possibility of a post-Marxist feminism that, instead of being inscribed in an affirmative ontology of power [*potencia*], is taken up from the tradition of theorizing negativity.

11 We refer to various debates that have emerged within progressive political organizations, between Latin American and European writers. For more on this debate, we recommend the collective book *A Feminism of the 99%* (2018), and the article by Clara Serra Sánchez, Justa Montero, Xulio Ferreiro, Ángela Rodríguez-Pam, and Silvia López Gil, "Feminización de la política" (2016), as well as the view of the crisis of care that Nancy Fraser proposes in her article "Contradictions of Capitalism and Care" (2016). But we also recommend recovering a series of classic debates in Latin American feminism that considered an emancipatory link between care and institutions, by authors such as Marta Lamas, Luisa Femenías, Sueli Carneiro, Lélia Gonzalez, and Sonia Álvarez, synthesized by

Alba Carosio in her text "Latin American feminism: ethical imperative for emancipation" (Carosio, 2009).

12 We refer here to the affirmative communitarian feminisms and post-Marxist feminisms mentioned above.

13 While we discussed these assumptions in Essay 3 in our exploration of the limits of autonomism, here we are interested in briefly returning to these problems from the perspective of the feminism that we hope to explore.

14 To say "the other of the self" is not to say "the other of the same," but nor is it, as feminists of sexual difference would argue, "the other of the other."

15 The first Not One Less march took place on June 3, 2015, simultaneously across different cities in Argentina, although its epicenter was in the Plaza del Congreso in Buenos Aires. Cristina Fernández de Kirchner used the phrase "The Homeland is the Other" in 2013 in a speech referring to solidarity actions by populist militants in the face of serious flooding in the city of La Plata in Buenos Aires province.

Bibliography

Alemán, Jorge (2009), *Para una izquierda lacaniana, Intervenciones y textos*, Buenos Aires: Grama Ediciones.

Alemán, Jorge (2014a), *Para una izquierda lacaniana ... Intervenciones y textos*, Buenos Aires: Grama Ediciones.

Alemán, Jorge (2014b), *En la frontera. Sujeto y capitalismo. El malestar en el presente neoliberal. Conversaciones con María Victoria Gimbel*, Buenos Aires: Gedisa.

Alemán, Jorge (2016), *Horizontes neoliberales en la subjetividad*, Buenos Aires: Grama Ediciones.

Alemán, Jorge (2019), *Capitalismo. Crimen perfecto o emancipación*, Buenos Aires: Nuevos Emprendedores Editoriales.

Althusser, Louis (2006), "Marx in his Limits," in *Philosophy of the Encounter: Later Writings, 1978–87*, London: Verso Books, pp. 7–162.

Althusser, Louis (2011), *Machiavelli and Us*, London: Verso.

Álvarez, Sonia E. (1998), "Los feminismos latinoamericanos se globalizan en los noventas: retos para un nuevo milenio," in M. L. Tarrés Barraza (ed.), *Género y cultura en América Latina*, Vol. I, Mexico City: El Colegio de Mexico, pp. 89–134.

Arditi, Benjamín (2003), "Populism, or, Politics at the Edges of Democracy," *Contemporary Politics*, 9, 1, pp. 17–31.

Arditi, Benjamín (2005), "Populism as Spectre of Democracy: A Response to Canovan," *Political Studies*, 52, pp. 135–46.

Badie, Bertrand, and Guy Hermet (1993), *Política comparada*, Mexico City: Fondo de Cultura Económica.

Barros, Sebastián (2005), "The Discursive Continuities of the Menemist Rupture," in F. Panizza (ed.), *Populism and the Mirror of Democracy*, London: Verso.

Bastian Duarte, A. (2012), "From the Margins of Latin American Feminism: Indigenous and Lesbian Feminisms", *Signs: Journal of Women in Culture and Society*, 38 (1): 153–78.

Bataille, Georges (1985 [1933]), 'The Psychological Structure of Fascism', in Allan Stoekl (ed.), *Visions of Excess: Selected Writings, 1927–1939*, Minneapolis: University of Minnesota Press, pp. 137–60.

Bertomeu, María Julia (2005), "Republicanismo y propiedad," *Sin permiso*: www.sinpermiso.info/textos/republicanismo-y-propiedad.

Bertomeu, María Julia (2015), "Las raíces republicanas del mundo moderno" (unpublished).

Biglieri, Paula, and Gustavo Guille (2017), "The Deconstructivist Laclau," *The Undecidable Unconscious: A Journal of Deconstruction and Psychoanalysis*, 4: https://doi.org/10.1353/ujd.2017.0000.

Biglieri, Paula, and Gloria Perelló (eds.) (2007), *En el nombre del pueblo. La emergencia del populismo kirchnerista*, Buenos Aires: UNSAM Edita.

Biglieri, Paula, and Gloria Perelló (2011), "The Names of the Real in Laclau's Theory: Antagonism, Dislocation and Heterogeneity," *Filozofski vestnik* (Liubliana), 32, 2, pp. 47–64.

Biglieri, Paula, and Gloria Perelló (2012), *Los usos del psicoanálisis en la teoría de la hegemonía de Ernesto Laclau*, Buenos Aires: Grama Ediciones.

Biglieri, Paula, and Gloria Perelló (2016), "Populist Politics and Post-Marxist Theory," *Contemporary Political Theory*, 15, 3, pp. 324–9.

Biglieri, Paula, and Gloria Perelló (2019), "Problemas teóricos, problemas politicos," (unpublished), paper delivered at the conference "Derivas de una izquierda lacaniana. En torno a los textos de Jorge Alemán," Facultad de Filosofía y Letras, Universidad de Buenos Aires, April.

Blengino, Luis (2019), "'¿Qué hay de nuevo, viejo?' Populismo transnacional, nacionalismos autoritarios y neoliberalismo global" (unpublished), paper presented at the conference "Fascism? Populism? Democracy?" International Consortium of Critical Theory Programs, University of Brighton, January.

Braidotti, Rosi (1991), "The Subject in Feminism," *Hypatia*, 6, 2, pp. 155–72.

Braidotti, Rosi (2002), *Metamorphoses: Towards a Materialist Theory of Becoming*, Cambridge: Polity.

Braidotti, Rosi (2004), *Feminismo, diferencia sexual y subjetividad nómade*, Barcelona: Gedisa.

Braidotti, Rosi, and Judith Butler (1994), "Feminism by Any Other Name," *differences* 6, 2–3, pp. 27–61.

Brown, Wendy (2017), *Undoing the Demos, Neoliberalism's Stealth Revolution*, New York: Zone Books.

Butler, Judith (1990), *Gender Trouble: Feminism and the Subversion of Identity*, New York: Routledge.

Cadahia, Luciana (2011), "Revolucionar un concepto: la democracia radical en Laclau," in M. Cereceda and G. Velasco (eds.), *El pensamiento político de la comunidad, a partir de Roberto Esposito*, Madrid: Arena Libros, pp. 131–43.

Cadahia, Luciana (2017), "Espectrologías del populismo en Ecuador: materiales para una lectura renovada de la Revolución ciudadana," in *Revolución ciudadana: avances y retrocesos*, Quito : IAEN.

Cadahia, Luciana (2018), "La tragicidad del populismo: hacia una reactivación de su dialéctica," in L. Cadahia, V. Coronel, and F. Ramírez (eds.), *A contracorriente: materiales para una teoría renovada del populismo*, La Paz: Estado Plurinacional de Bolivia.

Cadahia, Luciana (2019), *El círculo mágico del Estado: populismo, feminismo y antagonismo*, Madrid: Lengua de Trapo.

Cadahia, Luciana, Valeria Coronel, and Franklin Ramírez (eds.) (2018), *A contracorriente: materiales para una teoría renovada del populismo*, La Paz: Estado Plurinacional de Bolivia.

Cadahia, Luciana, Valeria Coronel, Soledad Stoessel, and Julio Guanche (2020), "Hacia una nueva lógica del populismo: de la ruptura de las instituciones a la institucionalidad populista," *Recerca. Revista de Pensament i Anàlisi*, 25, 1, pp. 1–20.

Canelas, Manuel, and Íñigo Errejón (2013), "Las autonomías en Bolivia y su horizonte: un análisis politico," in *Ensayos sobre la Autonomía en Bolivia*, La Paz: Ministerio de Autonomías y Friedrich Ebert Stiftung, pp. 21–32.

Canovan, Margaret (1999), "Trust the People! Populism and the Two Faces of Democracy," *Political Studies*, 47, 1, pp. 2–16.

Carneiro, Sueli (2000), "Noircir le féminisme," *Nouvelles Questions Féministes*, 24, 2, pp. 27–32.

Carosio, Alba (2009), "Feminismo latinoamericano: imperativo ético para la emancipación," in A. Girón (ed.), *Género y globalización*, Buenos Aires: CLACSO, pp. 229–52.

Cielo, Cristina, and Cristina Vega (2015), "Reproducción, mujeres y comunes. Leer a Silvia Federici desde el Ecuador actual," *Revista Nueva Sociedad*, 256, pp. 132–44.

Copjec, Joan (2002), *Imagine There's No Woman: Ethics and Sublimation*, Cambridge, MA: MIT Press.

Coronel, Valeria, and Luciana Cadahia (2018), "Populismo republicano: más allá de 'Estado versus pueblo,'" *Nueva Sociedad*: http://nuso.org/articulo/populismo-republicano-mas-alla-de-estado-versus-pueblo.

Curiel, Ochy (2007), "Crítica poscolonial desde las prácticas políticas del feminismo antirracista," *Nómadas*, 26, pp. 92–101.

Curiel, Ochy (2016), "Rethinking Radical Anti-Racist Feminist Politics in a Global Neoliberal Context," *Meridians*, 14, 2, pp. 46–55.

De Cleen, Benjamin, Benjamin Moffitt, Panos Panayotu, and Yannis Stavrakakis (2019), "The Potentials and Difficulties of Transnational Populism: The Case of the Democracy in Europe Movement 2025 (DIEM25)," *Political Studies*, 1–21: https://doi.org/10.1177/0032321719847576.

De Cleen, Benjamin, and Yannis Stavrakakis (2017), "Distinctions and Articulations: A Discourse Theoretical Framework for the Study of Populism and Nationalism," *Javnost, The Public*, 24, 4, pp. 301–19: https://doi.org/10. 1080/13183222.2017.1330083.

De Ípola, Emilio (2009), "La última utopía. Reflexiones sobre la teoría del populismo de Ernesto Laclau," in C. Hilb (ed.), *El político y el científico. Homenaje a Juan Carlos Portantiero*, Buenos Aires: Siglo XXI, pp. 197–220.

De Ípola, Emilio, and Juan Carlos Portantiero (1981), "Lo nacional popular y los populismos realmente existentes," *Nueva Sociedad*, 54, pp. 5–6.

De Ípola, Emilio, and Juan Carlos Portantiero (1982), "Populismo e ideología (A propósito de Ernesto Laclau: 'Política e ideología en la teoría marxista')," *Revista Mexicana de Sociología*, 41, 3, pp. 925–60.

De la Torre, Carlos (2000), "El fantasma del populismo está de vuelta," in M. Aguirre (ed.), *Controversias Ecuador hoy: cien miradas*, Quito: Flacso-Ecuador, pp. 204–6.

De la Torre, Carlos (2013), "El tecnopopulismo de Rafael Correa: ¿Es compatible el carisma con la tecnocracia?" in F. Álvarez González et al. (eds.), *El correísmo al desnudo*, Quito: Montecristi Vive, pp. 39–52.

De la Torre, Carlos (2015), *De Velasco a Correa: insurrección, populismos y elecciones en Ecuador, 1944–2013*, Quito: Corporación Editora Nacional y Universidad Andina Simón Bolívar.

De la Torre, Carlos, and E. Peruzzotti (eds.) (2008), *El retorno del pueblo: populismo y nuevas democracias en América Latina*, Quito: FLACSO-Ecuador y Ministerio de Cultura del Ecuador.

Di Tella, Torcuato (1965), "Populism and Reform in Latin America," in Claudio Véliz (ed.), *Obstacles to Change in Latin America*, Oxford University Press, pp. 47–74.

Domènech, Antoni (2004), *El eclipse de la fraternidad. Una lectura republicana de la tradición socialista*, Barcelona: Crítica.

Errejón, Íñigo (2013), "Sin manual, pero con pistas. Algunas trazas comunes en los procesos constituyentes andinos

(Venezuela, Bolivia y Ecuador)," *Vientos del Sur*, 128, pp. 27–37.

Espinosa Miñoso, Yuderkys (2011), "The Feminism–Lesbianism Relationship in Latin America: A Necessary Link," in J. Corrales and M. Pecheny (eds.), *The Politics of Sexuality in Latin America*, University of Pittsburgh Press, pp. 401–5.

Fassin, Éric (2018a), *Populismo de izquierdas y neoliberalismo*, Barcelona: Herder.

Fassin, Éric (2018b), "Left-wing Populism. A Legacy of Defeat: Interview with Éric Fassin": www.radicalphilosophy.com/article/left-wing-populism.

Femenías, María Luisa (2007), "Esbozo de un feminismo latinoamericano", *Estudios Feministas*, 15, 1, pp. 11–25.

Fernández-Liria, Carlos (2016), *En defensa del populismo*, Madrid: Catarata.

Foucault, Michel (2010), *The Birth of Biopolitics: Lectures at the Collège de France, 1978–1979*, New York: Picador.

Fraser, Nancy (2016), "Contradictions of Capitalism and Care," *New Left Review*, 100, 99–117.

Fraser, Nancy (2018), "Prólogo," in *Un Feminismo del 99%*, Madrid: Traficantes de Sueños.

Freud, Sigmund (1989a [1930, 1929]), *Civilization and its Discontents*, New York: Norton.

Freud, Sigmund (1989b [1901]), *The Psychopathology of Everyday Life*, New York: Norton.

Freud, Sigmund (1990a [1913–14]), *Totem and Taboo*, New York: Norton.

Freud, Sigmund (1990b [1920–2]), *Group Psychology and the Analysis of the Ego*, New York: Norton.

Gago, Verónica (2017). *Neoliberalism from Below: Popular Pragmatics and Baroque Economies*, Durham: Duke University Press.

Gago, Verónica (2020), *Feminist International: How to Change Everything*, London: Verso Books.

Gago, Verónica, and Sandro Mezzadra (2015), "Para una crítica de las operaciones extractivas del capital," *Nueva Sociedad*, 255, pp. 38–52: https://nuso.org/media/articles/downloads/4091_1.pdf.

Galindo, María (2004), *Las exiliadas del neoliberalismo*, La Paz: Mujeres Creando.

García Linera, Álvaro (2008), *La potencia plebeya. Acción colectiva e identidades indígenas, obreras y populares en Bolivia*, Buenos Aires: CLACSO/Prometeo.

Gargallo, Francesca (2006), *Ideas feministas latino-americanas*, Mexico City: UACM.

Germani, Gino (1968 [1956]), *Política y sociedad en una época de transición*, Buenos Aires: Ediciones Paidós.

Germani, Gino (2019), *Authoritarianism, Fascism, and National Populism*, London: Routledge.

Ginzburg, Carlo (2013), *Clues, Myths, and the Historical Method*, Baltimore: Johns Hopkins University Press.

Glynos, Jason, and Yannis Stavrakakis (2004), "Encounters of the Real Kind: Sussing Out the Limits of Laclau's Embrace of Lacan," in S. Critchley and O. Marchart (eds.), *Laclau: A Critical Reader*. London: Routledge, pp. 201–16.

Gonzalez, Lélia (2015), "La catégorie politico-culturelle d'amefricanité," *Les cahiers du CEDREF*, 20: http://journals.openedition.org/cedref/806.

Gramsci, Antonio (1998), *Literatura y vida nacional*, Mexico City: Juan Pablo Editor.

Guanche, Julio César (2018), "Disputas entre populismo, democracia y régimen representativo: un análisis desde el corporativismo en la Cuba de los 30," in L. Cadahia, V. Coronel, and F. Ramírez (eds.), *A contracorriente: materiales para una teoría renovada del populismo*, La Paz: Estado Plurinacional de Bolivia, pp. 59–80.

Gutiérrez Aguilar, Raquel (2017), *Horizontes comunitario-populares*, Madrid: Traficantes de Sueños.

Ionescu, Ghita, and Ernest Gellner (1970), *Populismo: sus significados y características nacionales*, Buenos Aires: Amorrortu.

Irigaray, Luce (1985a), *This Sex Which Is Not One*, Ithaca: Cornell University Press.

Irigaray, Luce (1985b), *Speculum of the Other Woman*. Ithaca: Cornell University Press.

Irigaray, Luce (1993), *Je, tu, nous: Towards a Culture of Difference*. London: Routledge.

Irigaray, Luce (2000), *To Be Two,* London: Routledge.

James, C. L. R. (2001), *The Black Jacobins: Toussaint L'Ouverture and the San Domingo Revolution,* New York: Penguin.

Lacan, Jacques (2005 [1953]), "The Function and Field of Speech and Language in Psychoanalysis," in *Écrits: A Selection,* New York: Norton, 2004, pp. 31–106.

Lacan, Jacques, (1998 [1964]), *The Seminar of Jacques Lacan: The Four Fundamental Concepts of Psychoanalysis* (Book 11), New York: Norton.

Lacan, Jacques (1999 [1972–3]), *The Seminar of Jacques Lacan: On Feminine Sexuality, the Limits of Love and Knowledge, 1972–1973* (Book 20), New York: Norton.

Laclau, Ernesto (1977), "Toward a Theory of Populism," in *Politics and Ideology in Marxist Theory: Capitalism, Fascism, Populism,* London: New Left Books, pp. 143–98.

Laclau, Ernesto (1990), *New Reflections on the Revolution of Our Time,* London and New York, Verso.

Laclau, Ernesto (2002), *Misticismo, retórica y política,* Mexico City: Fondo de Cultura Económica.

Laclau, Ernesto (2005a), *On Populist Reason,* London and New York: Verso.

Laclau, Ernesto (2005b), "Populism: What's in a Name?" in F. Panizza (ed.), *Populism and the Mirror of Democracy,* London and New York: Verso, pp. 32–49.

Laclau, Ernesto (2008), *Debates y combates. Por un nuevo horizonte de la política,* Buenos Aires: Fondo de Cultura Económica.

Laclau, Ernesto, and Judith Butler (1997), "The Uses of Equality," *Diacritics,* 27, 1, pp. 2–12.

Laclau, Ernesto, and Chantal Mouffe (1985), *Hegemony and Socialist Strategy: Towards a Radical Democratic Politics,* London and New York: Verso.

Lasso, Marixa ((2007), *Myths of Harmony: Race and Republicanism during the Age of Revolution, Colombia 1795–1831,* University of Pittsburgh Press.

Lazzarato, Maurizio (2019), "From Pinochet to Bolsonaro and Back Again" (unpublished), paper presented at the conference "Fascism? Populism? Democracy?" International Consortium of Critical Theory Programs, University of Brighton, January.

Le Bon, Gustave (1896), *The Crowd: A Study of the Popular Mind*, London: T. Fisher Unwin.

Lipset, Seymour M. (1960), *Political Man: The Social Bases of Politics*, New York: Doubleday.

Lugones, María (2011), "Hacia un feminismo descolonial," *La manzana de la discordia*, 6, 2: 105–19.

Machiavelli, Niccolò (1996), *Discourses on Livy*, University of Chicago Press.

Machiavelli, Niccolò (2003), *The Prince*, New York: Penguin.

Marchart, Oliver (2006), "En el nombre del pueblo: La razón populista y el sujeto de lo politico," *Cuadernos del CENDES* [Caracas: Universidad Central de Venezuela], 23, 62 (May–August), pp. 37–58.

Marchart, Oliver (2007), *Post-Foundational Political Thought: Political Difference in Nancy, Lefort, Badiou and Laclau*, Edinburgh University Press.

Marchart, Oliver (2018), *Thinking Antagonism: Political Ontology after Laclau*, Edinburgh University Press.

Mariátegui, José Carlos (1921), "La prensa Italiana," *El Tiempo* [Lima], 10 July: www.marxists.org/espanol/mariateg/oc/cartas_de_italia/paginas/la%20prensa%20italiana.htm.

Mariátegui, José Carlos (1971), *Seven Interpretive Essays on Peruvian Reality*, Austin: University of Texas Press.

Mariátegui, José Carlos (2010 [1923]), "Decimoquinta conferencia: Internacionalismo y Nacionalismo," in H. Alimonda, *La tarea americana*, Buenos Aires: CLACSO/Prometeo, pp. 235–42.

Mariátegui, José Carlos (2011 [1924]), "Nationalism and Internationalism," in H. E. Vanden and M. Becker (eds.), *An Anthology*, New York: Monthly Review, pp. 259–64.

Matos, Marlise, and Clarisse Paradis (2013), "Los feminismos latinoamericanos y su compleja relación con el Estado: debates actuals," *Íconos. Revista de Ciencias Sociales*, 45, pp. 91–107.

Mezzadra, Sandro, and Verónica Gago (2017), "In the Wake of the Plebeian Revolt: Social Movements, 'Progressive' Governments, and the Politics of Autonomy in Latin America," *Anthropological Theory*, 17, 4, pp. 474–96.

Modonesi, Massimo, and Maristella Svampa (2016), "Post-progresismo y horizontes emancipatorios," *La izquierda*

Diario: www.laizquierdadiario.com/Posprogresismo-y-horizo ntes-emancipatorios-en-America-Latina.

Monterroso, Augusto (2013), *El paraíso imperfecto. Antología tímida*. Spain: Editorial Debolsillo.

Mouffe, Chantal (1991), "Hegemonía e ideología en Gramsci," in *Antonio Gramsci y la realidad colombiana*, Foro Nacional por Colombia.

Mouffe, Chantal (1993), *The Return of the Political*, London and New York: Verso Books.

Mouffe, Chantal (2018), *For a Left Populism*, London and New York: Verso Books.

Mudde, Cas, and Cristóbal Rovira Kaltwasser (2013), "Exclusionary vs. Inclusionary Populism: Comparing Contemporary Europe and Latin America," *Government and Opposition*, 48, 2 (April), pp. 147–174.

Murmis, Miguel, and Juan Carlos Portantiero (1971), *Estudios sobre los orígenes del peronismo*, Buenos Aires: Siglo XXI.

Negri, Antonio (1999), *Insurgencies: Constituent Power and the Modern State*, Minneapolis: University of Minnesota Press.

Negri, Antonio (2000), *The Savage Anomaly: The Power of Spinoza's Metaphysics and Politics*, Minneapolis: University of Minnesota Press.

Negri, Antonio (2008), *Reflections on Empire*, Cambridge: Polity.

Negri, Antonio (2013), *Spinoza for Our time: Politics and Postmodernity*, New York: Columbia University Press.

Panizza, Francisco (2005), *Populism and the Mirror of Democracy*, London and New York: Verso Books.

Perelló, Gloria (2017), "Causa, necesidad y contingencia, algunas implicaciones políticas," *Memorias. IX Congreso Internacional de Investigación y Práctica Profesional en Psicología, Buenos Aires, Facultad de Psicología, Universidad de Buenos Aires*, 4, pp. 242–6.

Perelló, Gloria, and Biglieri, Paula (2012), "On the Debate around Immanence and Transcendence: Multitude or the People," *Cultural Studies*, 26, 2–3, pp. 319–29: http://dx.doi.org/10.1080/09502386.2011.647645.

Perelmiter, Luisina (2016). *Burocracia plebeya. La trastienda de la asistencia social en el Estado argentino*, Buenos Aires: Universidad Nacional de San Martín.

Pettit, Philip (1999), *Republicanism: A Theory of Freedom and Government*, Oxford University Press.

Preciado, Paul (2002). *Manifiesto Contra-Sexual*, Madrid: Opera Prima.

Preciado, Paul (2016). *Manifiesto contrasexual*, Barcelona: Anagrama.

Ramos, Jorge Abelardo (2006 [1957]), *Revolución y contrarevolución en la Argentina*, Buenos Aires: Secretaría Parlamentaria, Dirección de Publicaciones, Senado de la Nación.

Ramos, Jorge Abelardo (2011 [1968]), *Historia de la nación latinoamericana*, Buenos Aires: Peña Lillo, Ediciones Continente.

Raventós, Daniel (2005), "Propiedad, libertad republicana y Renta Básica de ciudadanía," *Polis. Revista Latinoamericana*, 10.

Retamozo, Martín, and Soledad Stoessel (2014), "El concepto de antagonismo en la teoría política contemporánea," *Estudios Políticos*, 44, pp. 13–34.

Rich, Adrienne (1994), "Notes Toward a Politics of Location," in *Blood, Bread, and Poetry: Selected Prose, 1979–1985*. New York: Norton, pp. 210–32.

Rinesi, Eduardo (2015), "Populismo y republicanism," *Revista Ensambles*, 2/3, pp. 84–94.

Rinesi, Eduardo (2018), "Populismo, democracia y república," in L. Cadahia, V. Coronel, and F. Ramírez (eds.), *A contracorriente: materiales para una teoría renovada del populismo*, La Paz: Estado Plurinacional de Bolivia, pp. 3–20.

Rinesi, Eduardo, and Matías Muraca (2010), "Populismo y república. Algunos apuntes sobre un debate actual," in *Si este no es el pueblo. Hegemonía, populismo y democracia*, Buenos Aires: Universidad General Sarmiento, pp. 59–73.

Rivera Berruz, Stephanie (2018), "Latin American Feminism," *Stanford Encyclopedia of Philosophy*: https://171.67.193.20/entries/feminism-latin-america.

Rivera Cusicanqui, Silvia (2018), *Un mundo ch'ixi es posible. Ensayos desde un presente en crisis*, Buenos Aires: Tinta Limón.

Sanders, James E. (2004), *Contentious Republicans: Popular Politics, Race, and Class in Nineteenth-Century Colombia*, Durham: Duke University Press.

Scott, Joan (1986), "Gender: A Useful Category of Historical Analysis," *American Historical Review*, 91, 5, pp. 1053–75.

Segato, Rita (2013), "Género y colonialidad: del patriarcado comunitario de baja intensidad al patriarcado colonial moderno de alta intensidad," in *La crítica del colonialidad en ocho ensayos y una antropologiá de la demanda*, Buenos Aires: Prometeo.

Serra Sánchez, Clara, Justa Montero, Xulio Ferreiro, Ángela Rodríguez-Pam, and Silvia López Gil (2016), "Feminización de la política," *La circular*: www.lacircular.info/index. html%3Fp=781.html.

Skinner, Quentin (1978), *The Foundations of Modern Political Thought*, Cambridge University Press.

Skinner, Quentin (1981), *Machiavelli*, Oxford University Press.

Stavrakakis, Yannis (2007), *The Lacanian Left: Psychoanalysis, Theory, and Politics*, Edinburgh University Press.

Stavrakakis, Yannis (2017), "Discourse Theory in Populism Research: Three Challenges and a Dilemma," *Journal of Language and Politics*, 16, 4, pp. 523–34: http://dx.doi. org/10.1075/jlp.17025.sta.

Stavrakakis, Yannis, and Giorgos Katsambekis (2015), "El populismo de izquierda en la periferia europea: el caso de Syriza," *Debates y Combates*, 5, 7, pp. 153–92.

Stoessel, Soledad (2014), "Los claroscuros del populismo. El caso de la Revolución Ciudadana en Ecuador," *Pasajes*, 46: http://roderic.uv.es/handle/10550/48916.

Taine, Hippolyte (1878), *Les origines de la France contemporaine*. La Révolution: I – l'Anarchie, Paris: Librairie Hachette.

Torres Santana, Ailynn (2018), "Signos y realizaciones republicanas en América Latina: líneas gruesas para el diálogo con los populismos," in L. Cadahia, V. Coronel, and F. Ramírez (eds.), *A contracorriente: materiales para una teoría renovada del populismo*, La Paz: Estado Plurinacional de Bolivia, pp. 21–42.

Vega Solís, Cristina (2009), *Culturas del cuidado en transición. Espacios, sujetos e imaginarios en una sociedad de migración*, Barcelona: Universitat Oberta de Catalunya.

Vilas, Carlos (1995), *La democratización fundamental: el populismo en América Latina,* Mexico City: Consejo Nacional para la Cultura y las Artes.

Vilas, Carlos (2009), "Populismo y democracia en América Latina: convergencias y disonancias": http://cmvilas.com.ar/index.php/articulos/15-populismos/15-populismo-y-democracia-en-america-latina-convergencias-y-disonancias.

Villacañas, José Luis (2015), *Populismo*, Madrid: La Huerta Grande.

Wittig, Monique (1985), "The Mark of Gender," *Feminist Issues*, 5, 2, pp. 3–12.

Worsley, Peter (1969), "The Concept of Populism," in G. Ionescu and E. Gellner (eds.), *Populism: Its Meanings and National Characteristics*, London: Weidenfeld and Nicolson.

Zanatta, Loris (2015), *El populismo*, Madrid: Katz.

Zapata, Francisco (1990), *Ideología y política en América Latina*, Mexico City: El Colegio de México.

Žižek, Slavoj (1990), "Beyond Discourse-Analysis," in E. Laclau, *New Reflections on the Revolution of Our Time*, London and New York: Verso, pp. 249–60.

Žižek, Slavoj (1991), *For They Know Not What They Do: Enjoyment as a Political Factor*, London: Verso Books.

Žižek, Slavoj (2009), "Why Populism Is (Sometimes) Good Enough in Practice, but Not in Theory," in S. Žižek, *In Defense of Lost Causes*, London and New York: Verso, pp. 264–333.

Žižek, Slavoj (2013), *Less Than Nothing: Hegel and the Shadow of Dialectical Materialism*, London and New York: Verso.

Žižek, Slavoj (2018), "Trump, como Perón, mezclan extremos," interview in *Diario Perfil*, www.perfil.com/noticias/periodismopuro/zizek-trump-como-peron-mezcla-extremos.phtml.

Index